What people are saying about …

MEET MRS. SMITH

"When you walk into Martin and Anna's house, whoever you are, you are made to feel a part of the family within about three seconds flat! They exude love, warmth, and acceptance from the minute you walk through the door, and this book is no different. I have to confess that I was totally hooked, and in the (few!) quiet moments between running around after three little ones, I found myself wanting to pick it up. *Meet Mrs. Smith* is funny, engaging, moving, profound, and incredibly cathartic for anyone who is part of a busy young family. Anna is characteristically honest, good-humored, and full of wisdom even as she shares some of their more testing times of the last decade. I would encourage *anyone* to read this book; there truly is something for everyone."

Rachel Hughes, wife of worship leader
and songwriter Tim Hughes

"I love Anna Smith, and I love reading about her story, her choices, and her heart. Over the years Anna has taught me so much about being a wife, a mum, and a woman of God. I know this bold and adventurous book will inspire and encourage you in the same way."

Beth Redman, singer, songwriter, and
author of *God Knows My Name*

MEET MRS. SMITH

MY ADVENTURES WITH SIX KIDS, ONE ROCKSTAR HUSBAND, AND A HEART TO FIGHT POVERTY

ANNA SMITH
AND CAROLYN JOHNSON

David C Cook®

transforming lives together

MEET MRS. SMITH
Published by David C Cook
4050 Lee Vance View
Colorado Springs, CO 80918 U.S.A.

David C Cook Distribution Canada
55 Woodslee Avenue, Paris, Ontario, Canada N3L 3E5

David C Cook U.K., Kingsway Communications
Eastbourne, East Sussex BN23 6NT, England

David C Cook and the graphic circle C logo
are registered trademarks of Cook Communications Ministries.

Unless otherwise noted, all Scripture quotations are taken from the Holy Bible, New International Version®, NIV®. Copyright © 1973, 1978, 1984 by Biblica, Inc™. Used by permission of Zondervan. All rights reserved worldwide. www.zondervan.com.

LCCN 2010940913
ISBN 978-1-4347-0203-6
eISBN 978-0-7814-0610-9

© 2011 Anna Smith

The Team: Alex Field, Amy Kiechlin, Sarah Schultz, Caitlyn York, Karen Athen
Cover Design: Mark Debnam
Cover Images: A photoshoot by Andy Hutchinson and iStockphoto, royalty-free

Printed in the United States of America
First Edition 2011

1 2 3 4 5 6 7 8 9 10

112910

This book is dedicated to my best friend and hubby,
Martin, and our little treasures: Elle-Anna, Noah,
Indi-Anna, Levi, Ruby-Anna, and Mary-Anna.
Also to Heather: my mum, friend, and inspiration.

CONTENTS

FOREWORD

I am sure that many of you reading this first knew of the Smiths through the beloved band Delirious?, and that was my story as well. But as I have *long* been fascinated with what is not seen immediately when it comes to people's lives ... I knew that behind these amazing worship musicians and prophets who were writing songs that were challenging our hearts to the core, there had to be some even more amazing wives at home, serving, loving, sacrificing, and making this all possible.

And I was right. All the women were (and are) incredible.... I knew that I had found friends for life. Enter Mrs. Anna Smith....

This gorgeous, talented, creative, funny, inclusive, godly, and compassionate dynamo has been fun to get to know from day one. Always with a child on her hip, high heels on, an arm extended to make you a coffee, heart open and engaged with you in the moment, Anna found her way into our hearts quickly and effortlessly, and our lives are so much richer for it.

But there is nothing like shared experiences to develop a long, lasting friendship, and we have had plenty of them thus far, both tragic and hilarious.

We initially bonded through prayer as I found myself joining the army of warriors who prayed for her fourth child, Levi, as he struggled with health problems as a baby. It's amazing how God brings people together! We have nervously giggled through the timing of contractions of baby number five's imminent arrival (as we dined in a castle, and as Martin momentarily lost the plot, and as my husband, Mark, drove as quickly as he could *home* … but it's a *long* story!); I have marveled as she has welcomed hundreds of people into her "open door" home to stay and be refreshed; we have cried through the loss of a child through miscarriage; we have dreamed together about what we could do to help relieve human suffering; I have met her on my doorstep as she has travelled with six tired children and one dreamy husband across the oceans to come to Australia; we have worshipped and prayed and spoken about the love of Christ till the sun came up.

And through it all she has never wavered in her commitment to Christ, her children, her marriage, her family and friends, her church, and her local community … and as she has been faithful, my family and I have watched in awe and delight as God continues to trust her with more.

I know that this book is going to be a great blessing and a great comfort to many, as Anna's writing style is so personable and warm that you will feel like you are sitting down and having a coffee with her—and to be honest, as a friend who lives on the other side of the planet from her, this is what I miss about her the most.

Be inspired as you read, and get to know my friend … the real Mrs. Smith.

Love,

Darlene Zschech

INTRODUCTION

The phone rings just as I'm straining the potatoes and promising the waiting tribe that supper's nearly ready.

"Indi, get back to the table.... Noah, try not to spill the water, my love.... Elle, can you encourage Levi not to arch his back in the high chair?"

Chaos.

I'm feeling slightly nauseous, and I wish the pregnancy hormones would take mealtimes into consideration—it's far too inconvenient for me to have my head down over the toilet right now. I hear ringing from the other room.

I rush to pick up the phone.

"*Helloooo,* Anna here."

"Hi, love, how are you?" Martin says.

"Yeah, good … general supper-time craziness, but we're all fine. How's your day been? What've you been up to?"

As he replies, I sense something different in Martin's voice tonight. I don't know, he seems bothered or troubled … *just different.* But there's no time to chat.

"Can't you phone in a couple of hours?" I ask him.

"Probably not," he replies. Later I guess that he'll be onstage or fast asleep in his hotel—I don't know; I get confused with the time zones. He starts to talk about everything he's experienced in India and how his heart's caving in at the poverty he's seeing.

What can I say?

"Sorry, honey, must be awful," I say. "Right, got to go, the broccoli's disintegrating."

My words sound pathetic. And I can't quite hear him anyway as the line is breaking up.

"Bye, I'll call again soon, I love you."

What horrible timing! As Martin wrestles with the impact of this great poverty he's seeing and experiencing, I'm here trying to hold down the fort. He's getting "all emotional" about someone else's kids, but all I can think of in that moment is how I need him here. Our children miss their daddy.

But every trip to India seems to ratchet up the intensity inside Martin—something's breaking his heart: He's moved, challenged, and provoked by everything around him there. *What's God saying? What's shifting?* Martin's seen poverty before, *but this is something else altogether.* It's another telephone call we'll have to resume later when the kids are in bed and my head's clearer.

The thing is, I want him in the kitchen with me now, pouring out his heart to me, like a proper married couple going on this journey of discovery *together*.

Not tonight though. He's somewhere in India, and I'm watching *Pop Idol* on TV.

We have been on a journey of so many paradoxes.

I'm on this adventure with my kids and my husband, Martin, who toured the world with the band Delirious? On this path I discovered both the joys and the chaos of family, but along the way, we found that our chaos was little compared to the chaos of the poverty in the world.

The clash of emotions and heartbreaking stories led my children and me to a rubbish dump, a slum where people live, outside Hyderabad, India.

What am I doing here? I thought as I stood there in the refuse and dirt. *Why did I bring my children to this place?* Then I saw the children run up to us with huge smiles on their beautiful faces—*and I wept when they sang to us.*

As I said before, this has been a journey of paradoxes.

The book in your hands is about this exhilarating, enriching, exciting, and downright exhausting journey. It's about being a wife, mother, friend, auntie, and sister. I'm a mother to six children, and due to that fact, it's a miracle that this book has actually been published and that I'm not yet wearing a hairnet to bed and putting my dentures in a plastic cup! Rather than wait until my life calms down, I want to tell someone my story while I am right in the middle of it.

This book is about not wishing away the time or waiting until the house is empty before we look out to the world beyond our own. It's about seeking God in all of the mess and exhaustion.

On this path, we look back on key events as turning points. For me, one of those moments came fifteen years ago. That moment accelerated my passion to embrace life to the fullest and birthed a band that played to hundreds of thousands of people around the world and spread a powerful message to the nations.

After three house moves, seven pregnancies, numerous flights with children in tow, many trips to India and Africa, dozens of tour buses, hundreds of gigs, thousands of earplugs in little ears, and too many dirty nappies (some might call them diapers!) to mention, I'm here to share a little of my story, from the sublime to the ridiculous.

Thanks for coming along!

—Anna

1

THE LONGEST NIGHT

Little did I know that one moment would change everything.

I sit motionless in the passenger seat. Frightened and disorientated, my muddled brain tries to make sense of my surroundings. Slowly I turn my head and look across at Martin lying semiconscious, his inert body collapsed in a heap next to me. His head is slumped against the steering wheel, his foot in perfect synchrony, pressed down flat on the accelerator.

I don't know what to do.

My head feels fuzzy and my thoughts move in slow motion.

At the time it seemed like a great idea to drive through the night. Waking up at home sounded sweet. There's nothing like your own bed, and after spending a week cooped up in a leaky caravan, sleeping under what I can only describe as soft cardboard, my bed called to me.

The green Ford Sierra did us proud, and the thought of seeing my sister's baby, Abigail, who'd been born ten days early (which was the motivation for our early departure), gave Martin and me lots to chat about on the way. My brother Jon fell asleep as soon as we left the campsite, so we had the whole journey to talk while eighties classics pumped out of our dilapidated stereo.

The A1 motorway continued on forever.

Martin had endured a hectic week, as part of his job was recording live music and seminars at conferences around the country, and this week we'd been at Grapevine in Lincolnshire. So it wasn't long before we'd exhausted all conversation and stared at the road, willing the journey to come to an end. Jon snoozed away in the back of the car—he looked peaceful, albeit a tad uncomfortable, curled up next to a load of musical equipment, trying to muster up an agreeable position with the seat belt across his face.

Five hours later we drove onto the A259 to Littlehampton. Waves of excitement came over me at the thought of seeing baby Abigail. I remember the delight of seeing the familiar Windmill Pub with the patrons long gone and the feeling that we were the only ones awake in this sleepy village. We were so nearly home.

The next few moments would change our lives forever, but the God who does not slumber watched over us.

My eyes photograph the scene. One by one, images develop to make sense of things: a green car turned the wrong way round; a crushed and crumbling brick wall; smoke swirling in the foreground; the driver motionless, covered in blood. My other senses start to kick into gear: Intoxicating fumes creep into my nostrils; the hiss and crackle of the engine whisper in my ear.

These impressions become clearer, and my thoughts accelerate— I *need* to get Martin and Jon out of the car. I desperately kick my chair back, but it stubbornly refuses to move. Every part of me clambers and scrambles to escape, but I can't get free.

"Someone call for help!" The words tumble out of my mouth and race into the cold night air, frantically searching for help.

Finally, I manage to force open my door. I tentatively step out of the car. My two-inch plastic heels crunch underfoot as fragments of glass break like icicles with every step.

I nervously survey the scene, but the dark gives nothing away. A ten-minute eternity passes. I wait, a thousand thoughts sparking a thousand fears. Suddenly, two fire engines and an ambulance careen around the corner, and the stillness is swallowed by a voracious urgency: lights and people, questions and confusion.

I'm ushered into the ambulance, the paramedics buzzing around me, assaulting my weary brain with questions. Jon somehow managed to get himself out of the car, but now he's dressed in a green surgical gown, hallucinating and singing "Yellow Submarine," the shock of it all messing with his reality.

But what about Martin—what about my husband?

Their answer is a constant, unsatisfying repetition: "We are doing all that we can."

The firefighters cut the roof off the car, the harsh grinding of metal against metal, battling to free the fragile body inside. I'm riveted to the action but can't watch—my heart needs protection, but my head doesn't want to miss any important detail. Fear and panic and emptiness and shock wrap around me like an oppressive shelter. Then in the midst of all the craziness, I see my dad running toward me, abandoned in panic. All I can think is that I need to tell him it's going to be all right. He holds me; he's shaking with fear, a thousand questions falling from his trembling lips.

The hours drag on heavily. People move around me in a haze, and nothing seems to change. I feel exhausted, confused, scared, and numb. The firefighters finally cut Martin free from the wreckage, and they are relieved to find that his feet are still attached to the legs that have been hidden from sight for two hours. Now that he's free, the paramedics are desperate to get him to the surgeon to repair his broken and battered body.

Blood is everywhere.

As we're leaving I hear one of the firefighters asking about the fourth passenger. *Where is she?* he asks. *The blonde girl in the backseat?*

To this day no one knows who she was. Either Jon had smuggled a new girlfriend home, or heaven made sure we weren't alone on this night.

Maybe she was our angel.

2
AT THE END
OF THE
WORLD

Plan your life like you will live forever, and live your life
like you will not see the next day.

—Anonymous

The long corridor of the hospital that leads to Chaffinch Ward is my
daily landscape. I pass artwork from the local high school and empty
trolleys nudged against the scuffed wall. As I walk along, the prayer
chapel on the left encourages me that I'm nearly at the end of this
long stretch. Only a few more plastic flap doors to negotiate, which
isn't easy when I'm juggling a handful of clean underwear, a plate of
grapes, books, and well-meaning cards and flowers.

It's been two weeks since Martin was admitted, and there's a
chance that he may be discharged by the weekend—*please, God, I
want him home!*

After Martin nearly lost his right foot, the surgeons inserted a
metal rod down the middle of his leg. Martin's recollection of that
night is still sketchy: He recalls relaxing as he drove, a mile away from

home. The next thing he remembers is wondering how on earth the dashboard landed in his lap.

I remember seeing him stare at his bloodstained fingers. Apparently, he was pleased that he still had all of them so at least he could play the guitar, even if he had no legs. The rest of my memory of that night is hazy. There was so much confusion and urgency, yet time seemed to drag as the shock left my body and the reality of the moment crystallised.

The hospital staff are amazing: professional, calm, and very approachable. Over the last few days I've been watching my husband scream in pain. It's horrible, and I feel so helpless knowing there's little I can do. It's been a low couple of weeks. Martin is insular, emotional, and depressed, and though I try to put on my happy, cheery, "everything's going to be alright" face, I often leave visiting hours feeling empty and lonely. I so badly want him to be able to come home, so we can get past this dark episode.

I've been staying with my parents since the crash because I need to be with people; otherwise I'll go crazy with worry. Mum's been a rock. She's one of life's incredibly strong and optimistic women: compassionate, full of humility, and extremely blessed with common sense. Yesterday, the enormity of the whole thing hit me; I got violently sick, then collapsed into sobbing and uncontrollable shaking. I've been trying to keep it together for two weeks, staying strong and positive, but I'm exhausted and my body is struggling with the shock of everything that's happened.

Today I walk through the last set of doors, feeling a bit flustered but trying to look ever so cool while walking past the ever-so-nice surgeon. It's time to put on a brave face as I walk into Martin's room.

"Hello, honey. How you doing today?"

Over those few weeks, I clocked up lots of visits to the hospital, and Martin lay on his bed with a few (hundred) minutes to spare. Among the flowers and cards, nurses and recovery routines, he started thinking about his life and what he was doing with it. Martin read the book *U2: At the End of the World* and couldn't put it down. The book lingered in his thoughts and stirred something inside him. He was inspired by a dream that came true for a bunch of Irish guys who touched the world with their music.

Alongside his studio and producing work, Martin was part of the house band for Cutting Edge, a local church youth gathering. One Sunday a month, Martin and the other band members, Tim Jupp (my eldest sister Becca's husband), Stew Smith (my next sister Sarah's husband), Jon (my younger brother), and Stu Garrard (a great friend, married to the beautiful Karen), led the music for the kids in town.

The band quickly became part of pioneering modern church worship, which led to them playing shows up and down the country while holding down day jobs. Somehow Martin knew God was speaking to him about taking the band to another level; about leaving their jobs and committing to the band full-time.

This required a huge step of faith.

Before each band member lay a life-changing choice, and, understandably, they were hesitant. They had three months to make their decision. Stew Smith worked as a successful graphic designer,

Tim owned a studio, Stu G was an electrician and session guitar player, Martin was a sound recording engineer, and Jon was still in art college.

This decision raised major questions for me. Martin became an emotional wreck—one day he was up, the next he was down. I didn't know what the drugs were doing, and I wanted him to take things slowly. But Martin grew adamant, fired up by an experience that taught him that life was a precious gift that should never be wasted. It felt strange as my husband developed this idea that was going to affect all these people. Suddenly, what had been a fun extracurricular activity outside our day-to-day lives had the potential to pull our close relationships even tighter, with friendships, family, careers, and commitments all merging into one project.

When the three months were up, they reached their verdict. Tim (keyboards and piano) sold his studio, Stew (drums) folded his design business, Jon (bass guitar) informed his tutor and quit college, Martin (vocals and guitar) left his job as a recording engineer, and Stu G (electric guitar) left his trade as an electrician.

Voila!

Delirious? was born.

Within months they got in the studio to record an album, and they set up a record label called Furious? Records. This was the birth of a rock band and the beginning of an incredible journey. For our family, this was the start of a new adventure that changed our lives forever—we had escaped death, and now life was for living.

August 30th

Thank you for the chance to live again
I will run always for you
Clouds had gathered all around my head
But these hands they lifted me
And I'll tell of this love that saved me

Thank you for the chance to live again
I will run always for you
Walking closer you are all I have in this world only you
And I'll tell of this love that saved me

And I'll wait for this light to break
I'll come to you, yes I'll run to you
And I'll wait for this light to break
I'll run to you, yes I'll come to you
I'll be one with you

Martin Smith, "August 30th," *King of Fools* © 1997 Curious? Music/Kingsway Music

3

GREAT VOICE, BAD SUIT

A regular event of my childhood was Spring Harvest, a weeklong church event held at a holiday resort. So, when I was sixteen I spent my Easter holiday working on my uncle Ishmael's team, providing hours of activities for children while their parents went to various talks and seminars. I wore yellow, jumped up and down enthusiastically to kids' songs, and generally had a great time with the children.

It was here that I met Martin. He worked for a recording studio, taping talks and music from the various sessions. During the week he'd become friends with Tim Jupp, who was engaged to Becca, so we were introduced but I was nothing more to him than his mate's fiancée's little sister.

Martin had a girlfriend at the time, and I was kissing Jamie Scott, stud muffin (later to marry my best mate, Tracy). To be honest I wasn't entertaining the idea of anything more than friendship at the time. I can't categorically say that I wasn't a teeny bit interested in him, but it was nothing too flirty, just an awkward girlie giggle and a flick of the hair now and again. He was a bit of a mystery man. Martin would sit in the corner with his long blond hair and pale denim jeans and talk about God. He was beautifully shy, and he intrigued me.

Our paths didn't cross again until Becca and Tim married two years later, and by that time I'd forgotten all about him. Martin sang at the wedding wearing a suit two sizes too big. My first conversation with him was along the lines of "great voice, bad suit."

When he turned twenty-one, he had a party and invited both my sisters but not me—so I was left at home watching the telly, and as a result he went down in my estimation.

Meanwhile, I pursued my dream to start a children's nursery in our local community. I wanted it full of colour with a carpeted play area that would make little eyes sparkle. Shortly after my eighteenth birthday the play centre became a reality, providing a nursery facility for up to fifteen children. I was deeply passionate about it, and unknown to me at the time, I would frequent the centre with my first, second, third, fourth, fifth, and sixth child for twenty years to come.

Martin redeemed himself a couple of weeks after the play centre opened, and we went on a date to The Three Cooks. No, this was not a rock 'n' roll band debuting at Wembley Stadium; rather, it was the village bakery!

We sat across the table from each other while he ate a bowl of watery leek and potato soup, with chips on the side, and I had a shrimp and mayo baguette. We sat frozen without much to say to each other. An awkward silence hung in the air. Thankfully the next date involved a little more dialogue.

Martin handed in his notice at his studio job in Eastbourne in April 1992, after five and a half years there, and started working with

Tim. He needed somewhere to live, so my dad invited him to live with us. (My dad would never have done this if he'd known that I was developing strong feelings for Martin!)

Becca freed up a bedroom when she married Tim, and the new lodger planned to move into the room in December. Martin was thin and pale and new in town; I think my mum wanted to fatten him up with a good plate of veggies. Meanwhile, he and I quietly fell in love. He was everything I wasn't: serious, thoughtful, and introverted, whereas I was outgoing, fun, and the life of the party. Things began to progress.

Martin moved into our home on the twentieth of December with a small suitcase and a lot of gratitude. The house was full of Christmas cheer—mince pies and a dollop of brandy sauce the daily dessert for the next couple of weeks. We enjoyed seeing so much of each other, and the Christmas-tree lights seemed to brighten when we were both in the room. However, neither of us entertained the notion of going out with each other while he lived in the house.

That idea didn't last long! On his second day living with us we watched one of those classic Christmas movies. One by one the family disappeared up to bed, but Martin and I stayed up chatting and giggling—there was some outrageous flirting happening behind the curtains in Jubilee Avenue. We were looking at the presents under the tree when his knees touched mine. It felt like a bolt of lightning through my veins! He helped me to my feet and grabbed me as I was approaching the door. We both knew that any kind of relationship was a bad idea and that we should really wait. But it wasn't easy being rational with my hormones raging and when everything within me was screaming, "Kiss me!"

Then he kissed me!

The next morning we all sat around the breakfast table, Martin and I catching each other's gaze and smiling. As we swapped glances over the table, I pretended to eat my cornflakes, stirring them round the bowl until they were too soggy for consumption. It was Saturday, so I ran off to work at Woolworth's, dressed to impress in my navy blue skirt and fetching striped shirt. I was glad to be hidden in the stationery aisle, stacking shelves, where I could relive the night before again and again in my mind, interrupted every now and again by shoppers wanting to know the location of the glue sticks or tape.

Martin headed off to his family home in Surrey for Christmas, waving good-bye and sending a wink my way in his rearview mirror. He called on Christmas morning to wish us all Merry Christmas and was a little miffed that I hadn't answered the phone.

However, after a few days, the cat was out the bag when he returned to our doorstep asking to see me. On New Year's Eve we escaped to the river and he presented me with a huge bouquet of flowers. I wore a red crushed-velvet dress with matching shoes (sounds hideous, but I was an eighties girl, what can I say!), and after spending the day together we celebrated at my uncle Ishmael's house.

As the clock struck twelve he asked if I would be his girl.

Of course I said "Yes!"

4

DIAMONDS ARE FOREVER

Marriage partners should be best friends. Valuable friendships are not found, they are built.

—Dave and Joyce Ames

Martin was my first *proper* boyfriend, and I surprised myself with how quickly I fell for this guy. The reason for my sparse collection of boys was that yours truly was extremely picky. Too short, too tall, bad skin, over keen, not keen enough—*the list went on.*

Martin didn't check off any of the boxes on my "future husband" list either. No one knew him. In fact, I didn't really know him myself, and even now sometimes I feel like I don't (so often with creative people, there is an elusive part that Mrs. Practical doesn't always understand).

I pasted pictures of hunky surf dudes on all my college folders, and the famous Athena print of the tough-but-tender man holding a baby adorned my bedroom. These were more my type, and here I was falling deeper in love. What would my mates say? What would my sisters think? Tim and Becca thought he was pretty amazing; Sarah wanted the best for me, so reserved judgment; and Mum and Dad loved him because he was a worship leader. And the more time I spent with him, the more he intrigued me. We were chalk and cheese, but opposites *do* attract, and our personalities complemented each other.

And there was undeniable chemistry.

One evening, he took me to see his parents, Eddie and Sylvia, for supper. I was riddled with nerves and held Martin's hand under the linen tablecloth. They couldn't have been more friendly and kind, and by the time the apple pie came out of the oven we were past the awkward first moments. Suzi, Martin's sister, was there, and we hit it off immediately: She danced and loved fashion, so we shared many common interests. I also met Martin's sister-in-law Pip, who was charismatic and warm. Pip commented at the dinner table that our children would have brown eyes, which I thought was making a huge assumption at the time, *but how right she was!* When it was time to go, we got in the car and Martin drove me home.

We dated for a year, and I started to think more and more about whether this was the man with whom I wanted to spend the rest of my life. My search was over; or was it? One moment I felt confident that he was the one, and the next moment I would panic and question it all. How can you be sure? I wouldn't dream of walking into a shoe shop and purchasing the first pair I tried on—I'd have to sample at least a half dozen in order to make an informed decision! And yet here I was, ready to spend the rest of my life with a man that I was crazy about but hardly knew.

My little brother Ben became the sounding board that I needed: too young to really care a hoot, but perfect for getting things off my

chest. Ben and I were very close. When he was born, I set about organising the whole event, seeing a chance to be a mum before my time.
Benjamin Peter Thatcher was born on the 12th of February 1988.
I saw him an hour after he was born, and from that moment on, I
doted on him. I loved spending time with him and would save up my
earnings from my Saturday job just to buy him clothes. As a toddler,
he loved to play with an array of saucepans and wooden spoons—so
it's hardly surprising that he is now an exceptional drummer.

So during this time, Ben and I would stroll into the village
together and buy two beef tomatoes from the greengrocers and then
walk until the first swing or bench became available. There I would
pour out my troubled thoughts and unanswered questions to a
seven-year-old, peachy, freckled face looking at me and nodding. He
always managed to finish his tomato first—*not surprisingly!*

In a short space of time, things progressed rapidly and soon we
were talking about marriage. We dashed into Brighton to choose a
ring, even though Martin hadn't popped the question yet. Together,
we gazed at the numerous diamonds glistening under the artificial
light. I was only nineteen and didn't really have a clue about what
cut or karat any of them were, and the ones that caught my eye had
too many zeros at the end of the price tag. So despite the overzealous
sales assistant we settled on a modest diamond that looked pretty on
my finger. I couldn't stop pulling it out of the box during the journey
home, much to my intended fiancé's disapproval. Secretly, he loved
it just as much as I did.

Martin kept the box and our trusted secret—we weren't going
to mention our plans to anyone. Two weeks later we were walking
along the beach on a warm September evening when I spotted an

umbrella in the distance. As we neared the umbrella, I became aware that it was for my benefit. Underneath the parasol was a rug with a candle, a rose, two champagne flutes, and some iced champers in a bucket resembling a metal flowerpot. Martin, a true gentleman, straightened up the rug and opened the champagne, and I prepared for the most romantic moment of my life.

There were two pops: one a cork (a bit premature as I hadn't said yes yet) and the other the question, which Martin had scribbled on a card: "Anna, will you spend the rest of your life with me?"

It didn't take long for me to say yes!

I was so excited and overwhelmed with a million thoughts and questions: *Did I really just say yes?! I can't wait to tell everyone! How many bridesmaids shall I have? What will people say? Is this crazy?*

The ring was on my finger and the embrace unrushed. By now the air was chilly, and the wind had picked up the parasol, carrying it toward East Preston. It was time to pack up and continue our celebrations elsewhere. Martin had reserved a table in a humble little Italian restaurant overlooking the castle in Arundel, a historic treasure in the heart of the West Sussex countryside.

We ate pizza and thought about the scale of the wedding—an intimate ceremony or an inclusive big bash? I had always envisaged a big wedding, and the guest list was already spilling onto the third paper napkin—and that was just our families.

But first we needed to tell everyone.

On my mother's birthday, the 18th of September, we announced our engagement by throwing a party at Martin's parents' house in Surrey. I invited all my pals from my neck of the woods, and Martin had his church youth group and music friends. That evening

Martin was flying in from another part of Europe, and his flight was inconveniently delayed. He arrived at the party by the skin of his teeth but got violently sick minutes after stepping through the front door. He spent the entire evening upstairs with a bowl by the bed, some flat lemonade, and a tea biscuit to nibble on. So with my fiancé feeling down, I celebrated our engagement on my own—everyone was there, so the party had to continue!

Every bride wants her perfect dress, and the search for mine began in earnest. I skipped into many a bridal shop with my sisters, bundling into the large dressing rooms with a pair of tights pulled over my face to stop my bright red lipstick from making its mark. I planned to pay for my dress myself and had been saving up from my Saturday job for ages. Then I found "the one," only it had a price tag that doubled my budget. I will never forget returning home from my shopping trip to find an envelope containing £200. The unsigned card simply read:

"To buy the dress of your dreams."

I was ecstatic.

Anonymous, you know who you are, and you really blessed me with your generosity, my friend.

In the evenings and during my spare minutes I cut snippets out of bridal magazines to present a montage of my favourite ideas. I became a productive and purposeful bee, and, in true community spirit, offers of help were plentiful. Pat Smith decorated the cake, Pat Evans decorated the hall, and Pat West made the bridesmaid dresses—three helpful women, all called Pat!

The fashion of the times was the "neutral" look: Beige, cream, white, and stone were on every wedding shop mannequin. Layers and linen were in vogue, as were Laura Ashley-style floaty dresses. But I wanted a splash of colour and sought out brightly themed decor. So I resisted the tasteful lilies and tulips in favour of a more cheerful flower: the gerbera. Fittings, fabrics, honeymoon brochures, and menus dominated my conversations. All my cousins, sisters, and brothers were in the bridal party, including Becca, who was five months pregnant and causing the dressmaker to do a lot of guesswork as to the size of her waist come July.

Alongside the necessary wedding arrangements were marriage preparation classes, whose intention was to equip us for every problem that might disrupt our harmonious relationship. The church leaders assigned this task were none other than my parents, which was wonderful when discussing conflict and communication, but awkward when answering questions about whether we would prefer to make love with the lights on or off—this was a topic discussed with minimal eye contact with my dad.

How embarrassing! Mum and Dad were sensitive and gave us the questions so Martin and I could discuss them in private. However, we bent the rules and opted out of the feedback sessions, favouring a bacon sandwich and a mug of hot chocolate instead.

The wedding date neared, and summer had arrived.

A woman needs ...

... someone who cares about her well-being, to understand what she is going through and recognise the validity of her feelings ... someone to love freely and trust that she will be loved in return ... someone to notice her, love her, and adore her ...

A man needs ...

... someone to accept him just the way he is ... someone to trust him and depend on him for what he can provide ... someone who admires him for what he has done or tried to do ... someone who gives him the opportunity to fulfill her needs ...

5

CONFETTI

Marriage is the acknowledgment that our partner is
special to us on all levels and that we are committed
to the growth of love in the relationship.

—John Gray

Travel and jet lag were going to be the highs and lows of our marriage journey, and it started even before the day itself. A week before the wedding, Martin flew to Jerusalem, not to voice last-minute wedding nerves at the Wailing Wall, but to record some songs. A record company had assigned him to record an album entitled *Israel Worships,* so he visited Israel to soak up the culture and visit synagogues to add authenticity to his project. With the material gathered and ready to produce, he flew back the night before our wedding rehearsal, cutting it close.

We turned up at the rehearsal not really in the frame of mind that we perhaps ought to have had. For a start, my father didn't like my T-shirt, which read, "Enjoy life to the full." Martin was jet-lagged and preoccupied by his recent visit to the Holy Land. And I giggled my way through the evening, hiding a tinge of nerves as we dutifully said the "I dos" and "I wills" in all the right places. The fourteen bridesmaids arranged their order of entrance, which took a while to arbitrate. By the time we had perfected the "one step, feet together, left foot, feet together, right foot" sequence, the music had run out for my grand entrance, so we abandoned the plan and had them walk behind me in quick march down the aisle!

The morning of 9 July 1994 was glorious—sun streamed through the windows, with a promising forecast. Temperatures soared, and I was tempted to do some last-minute sunbathing but thought better of it—a burnt face might not be a good look. Besides, there were many excitable bridesmaids to get ready, and although we'd scheduled a leisurely morning, I was well aware of how time could fly and didn't want to have to sprint down the aisle to meet my man.

The bedroom soon resembled a beauty parlor with hair rollers, makeup tubes, and nail-polish bottles lining every available surface. The concoction of perfumes was intense, enough to give anyone a migraine. A quick squirt of Dune in my hair was probably one too many—Martin was likely to smell me before he could see me! Hair dryers muffled out the background orchestral music, and all was busy in the house—a hive of productivity. Carina the hairdresser looked a little wide-eyed as she curled the fifth head of golden locks.

Mine was the penultimate head of hair to be completed, but halfway through my hairdresser was called to an emergency, leaving me to copy the other half of my head with a pair of tongs and a curling brush. That accomplished, I set to work on the final bridesmaid, my sister-in-law-to-be, Suzi. By the skin of our teeth, the bridal party looked divine, ready to pose for the first of hundreds of photographs. A bridal magazine wanted to print some shots of the occasion, so photographers were busy shooting close-ups of the flower girls and capturing their innocent beauty on camera.

Our budget was minimal, so I had made all the headdresses, using colourful tissue paper scrunched up like flower buds and sewn onto the garlands. Members of the church family I'd been part of all my life also helped make the day happen. While the woman with the gift of baking made the cake, the guy with the sports car drove me to the church. The hall was to be the venue for both the ceremony and reception; this meant a lot of behind-the-scenes action and speedy table-setting to make it ready for part two (luckily the photographer had a long list of family snapshots to plow through). The space was transformed from a school assembly room to a parade of vibrant colour. I hadn't been able to decide on a dual colour theme, so I brought in the lot—*every colour of the rainbow!* Flowers were too expensive, so we had balloons instead.

As I stood in the foyer with my dad, he squeezed my hand and told me how proud he was of me. It was formal, but heartfelt—the words any daughter wants to hear.

The music struck up, the congregation stood, and the procession began. Singer-songwriter and friend Cathy Burton was the first person I saw grinning at me. I felt like a celebrity in my satin and tulle gown. Becca followed me down the aisle, stepping on my veil and causing my head to jerk backward twice—but she was eight months pregnant, and she was forgiven.

The moment seemed to last forever. I walked down the aisle to an instrumental version of "What Is This Thing Called Love," a song Martin wrote for me. Once my dad walked me to the front, he turned around to lead the service. During his talk, my father told a story of how my sister had leaned back on a deck chair, unaware of the fact that my fingers were inside. The force of the chair chopped the nail completely off my wedding finger, and the doctor said it was unlikely to grow back. My father prayed that the nail would heal. As I stood there on my wedding day, my healed finger was a testimony to the wonder of God, who created the whole universe and was interested in the smallest details of my life, even down to the tip of my finger.

We exchanged rings, and when Martin was told that he "may kiss the bride," he embraced me, lifted me to my feet, and swung me round, accompanied by rapturous applause!

We had fruit punch and cake on the lawn while Auntie Mary and Uncle Michael cooked up a feast for the 250 guests to enjoy. After our last slow dance, we left our friends and family in the capable hands of the local DJ.

Our Ford Sierra (originally green, but on this day it was camou- flaged with toilet paper and whipped cream) gave one last hoot as we trailed off down the road, tin cans clattering behind us. None of this worried Martin too much—he just seemed incredibly focused on getting us to the hotel.

He muttered something about the day finishing with a *bang*, which kept us giggling uncontrollably all the way. We were both virgins on our wedding day, so the scenic route was *not* an option.

6

THE SHACK

We spent our first night in Bosham, a quaint estuary village west of Chichester. It was the first time we'd been away together, and it felt strange, if not awkward, that we were allowed to be on our own for the night. After an amazing day we were full of anticipation, tired, and hungry—but let's just say that dinner had to wait, for we had waited long enough.

Good night!

The next morning we strolled along the waterfront, working off a hearty breakfast, hand in hand as Mr. and Mrs. Smith—*and it felt so good to say that!* This was the beginning of the rest of our lives.

Looking back now, I realise that we got married after knowing each other for only two years, and found that the reality of doing life with someone is so much more about commitment than feelings. I fell in love with a mystery man, and I still don't know him completely—and probably never will. Martin enjoys having one foot in heaven, which is one of the things I love about him, but I can't pretend it doesn't drive me crazy at times!

Before we knew it we were at the airport and on the way to our "dream" holiday. After a four-hour flight, a significant amount of turbulence, and spaghetti bolognese that burnt the tip of my tongue, we landed in Turkey.

The haze of heat hit us the moment we exited the aircraft, as we breathed in the dry, warm air. We settled in for one week of uninterrupted sunbathing with not a table-seating plan in sight—*what bliss!* These days, when I holiday with six children, I remind myself of those wonderful moments of sheer indulgence. I remember closing my eyes without the fear of having to leap up, half my swimming costume coming adrift, in order to rescue a screaming child. I remember reading an entire article from my trashy celebrity magazine all the way through to the end! How times have changed!

Some people pay a fortune to have an exfoliation treatment, but we mothers get that for free, as sand is squished all over our tummies by sticky lollipop fingers!

The coach journey to Ölüdeniz was an hour-long endurance test of winding roads—the twists and turns turned my face varying shades of green. One by one the driver dropped other vacationers off at their plush resorts to start their week of unwinding. Finally, the driver brought us to a halt, called our names from his clipboard, and we nervously disembarked the coach.

Sometimes in life, things aren't always what they seem.

Sometimes our expectations overshoot reality and you wonder at which particular angle the photographer took the snapshot for the "Escape to Paradise" brochure. Arrival at our accommodation confirmed our worst fears: Our idyllic, secluded getaway was in fact *a glorified shed*.

We shunted our luggage across the cobbles and heaved the cases up the dusty track to our "hotel." Maybe the room would be a pleasant surprise, we thought, *or not!*

The windows were covered with chicken wire, the bedsheets grubby, and the gap under the door large to say the least—there was no point in worrying about cockroaches scuttling into our room (that was a given), but even the local stray cats would have had no trouble slipping through that crack under that door!

However, we were determined to have a good time, so we rolled our beach things in our towels and headed to the pool next door. We spent the majority of the first day horizontal. Hold on—I had better qualify that statement! We lay out in the sun, sipping cold drinks and relaxing after the busyness of the wedding—it felt good to be alone with my man, just him and me.

As we spent our first week together alone, I began to think of the future. *"Our" future.* I had to remind myself that we were two separate souls now living as one. I remember asking myself lots of questions. Would we make it together? So many marriages around us didn't seem to last; would we be the same? What if we were too different? Would Mart be a good dad? How many children would we have? We were both passionate about giving our lives to God, but what would that really mean for us? Even back then, lying blissfully by the pool, I had a feeling that our life together was not going to be normal and that there would somehow be a price to pay for all the dreams in our hearts.

Day two was a scorcher, and following the routine of the first day, we reserved our lounge chairs and spent the day soaking up the sun. One thing about Brits abroad is that they are *not* used to the sun. We think that we don't need suncream and that one cup of tea for breakfast is the only fluid we need on a hot day. Martin hadn't had enough water and so felt severely dehydrated—and, much to my amusement, nearly collapsed when we stood up to go.

Later that evening, he went to get a glass of water from reception, and Mr. Accident-Prone managed to faint before he got there, tripping over a table, falling headfirst into a rosebush, and cutting open his chin on the stone floor, which rendered him unconscious.

Oblivious to the fact that my husband was out cold, I continued reading my novel, but before I could get to the end of the chapter, a harassing waiter disturbed me by shouting and beckoning me to follow him to the lobby. He led me to the concierge desk where Martin sat with his hands cupping his chin, holding back the blood that was dripping onto the marble tiles. In sickness and in health—the vows were already coming into play. I helped Martin back to our room, but by 2:00 a.m. he was hallucinating so badly that in desperation I phoned reception to plead with them to get a doctor, who eventually came, stinking of alcohol and sweat. The language barrier was tricky to negotiate, so I tried to get by with hand gestures and speaking slowly. The doctor laid Martin on the bed, and after a brief examination proceeded to sew up his chin with surgical equipment that looked like a butcher's tool kit, and without a whiff of anesthetic. It was hideous to watch, and I can't begin to imagine what it was like on the receiving end.

Believe it or not, we managed to laugh it off, and I thought Martin looked quite fetching in his Speedo with a whopping big bandage across his chin! Needless to say, we skipped the camel ride, took it easy, and flew home a week later.

I knew then that life with Martin was always going to have a certain degree of drama. After all, I married a singer and a performer—I should have expected nothing less!

7

THRESHOLD

Our first home was nestled in a little village called East Preston, a five-minute drive from my parents' home. The two-bedroom apartment suited us perfectly, and we set to work with all the enthusiasm of new-lyweds in their first pad. I soon became aware of Martin's eccentricities and realised that his priorities for the house were far different from mine. While I picked out different paint colours, he cut two holes in the bathroom paneling for car speakers that would fill the bathroom with sonic delight. He spent hours laying speaker cables, soldering, and wiring, while I washed the floor (and not a lot has changed, to be honest!).

We converted a double divan into a four-poster bed using wood bought from the local lumberyard, and we painted over all the 1960s floral wallpaper. Then we opened the doors to all and sundry that wished to pop by—we loved having our own place in which to entertain.

What I remember about that home was the absence of children. It's bizarre to think it now, but we actually had two years of married life without kids. We slept in till midday, did what we wanted, ate meals together without interruption, and constantly felt tired. (It's amazing how many people without kids say they're exhausted all the time—now I think it would feel like being permanently at the spa!) To this day our front door is rarely shut for too long, and looking back, this was the beginning of many parties, laughter, fun, and thousands of cups of tea.

Martin had already started travelling with the band, playing most Fridays and Saturdays in different towns and cities around the UK. From the very beginning of our marriage it was obvious that Martin had a clear calling and a mission on his life. It was quite simple, really—when he sang, the light inside people switched on, whether in a small church or a big arena. I was just the "play centre" girl who looked after kids, and at times I felt like a passenger who couldn't reach the brake in a car going too fast.

I did find it difficult at times that our weekends were nonexistent and that our day off together was Monday when I was at work. Staying strong and staying together on our journey was often a struggle. Sometimes we craved time to just stare into each other's eyes. Inevitably, as the band became more successful we had to fight for moments together and time with God. Our local church was a constant part of our lives and community. The guys would always try to drive back through the night to be at church Sunday morning. That community was and still is a huge priority for us, and in a marriage without any proper rhythm it created a solid foundation on which to build our lives.

Martin seems to adore most things about me, but he's quick to flag my lack of culinary skills. The poor bloke has lived on pasta bake for most of our married life, and I still seem to burn part of whatever I serve up. Sometimes I've completely forgotten to cook anything. On one occasion, I invited Martin's mum and dad around for dinner and realised I only had a box of breakfast cereal in the cupboard. Thankfully, they ate it politely, even commenting on how tasty it was! Martin sometimes looks forward to getting on a plane because he knows he's going to get a good meal, even if he has to eat it out of a cardboard tray. So please feel free to pop by the house; there may not be any food, but we've always got chocolates and sweets!

A couple of years passed, and life bumbled along. I thoroughly enjoyed life at my children's play centre as Martin produced records for our songwriter friend Matt Redman.

After the car crash, many things began to change. That event was a wake-up call that opened Martin's eyes to new possibilities. That night was momentous in so many ways, and we are incredibly thankful to God that He protected us and provided for us through the whole experience. He brought us out the other side and encouraged us to go on a new adventure.

Martin's career quickly began to take a different path, and we decided to move into our first house, around the corner in the village of Rustington. To bring some relief to the whole ordeal of the accident, Martin whisked me away to Paris for a long weekend, which was a great tonic and time to unwind. Romantic? Yes. Expensive? Very. On day two we went to McDonald's, as it was all we could afford! We hobbled around the streets (Martin with his walking cane) and indulged in the cafés and street markets and had our portrait sketched by a street artist.

Inspired by our romantic trip, we called our new home Montmartre, and my mum, my good friend Polly, and I, dusters in hand, transformed this house into a home within days.

Strangely, though, it now felt like something was missing. Could it be time for the patter of little feet?

No problem is too big for God. If it is, we need to make God bigger and watch the problem shrink. Small God, big problem—big God, small problem.

8

A BLUE LINE

Like many couples, we naively thought having children would be a piece of cake. Ready to start a family early on in our marriage, we expected it to happen right away. Not so. It was 1996, and I was twenty-two, and month after month nothing happened.

Both my sisters got pregnant quickly, and I assumed I would follow suit. Six months passed, and still nothing. It felt like we were waiting forever, and it crossed my mind that maybe we wouldn't be able to have children. The words *barren* and *infertile* crept into my subconscious, trying to steal my hope. In my private moments, I would surrender to God's promise, standing on the truth of His word that He will give us the desires of our hearts, and in doing so I had to take control of the negative thoughts. Irrespective of how I was feeling, I had to rise above my circumstances and trust God.

In the great scheme of things, six months was no time at all. I have many friends who have waited earnestly and patiently, and indeed are still waiting, *far longer than I did.* We've got friends who haven't been able to have children, and this has caused us all so much pain on many levels and has left us asking why and whether God cares. There are so many questions in life that are unanswerable—which leaves us with unsolvable mysteries or divine silences. There are so many times when we feel that God has gone on holiday and left us home alone, abandoned by someone who is supposed to be good. I have wept with my girlfriends, sat in silence through the tears, and not understood why some people can easily have children and others just can't. At times like this we sometimes question God's existence, but faith is there for the good and the bad times, for when we don't understand and when our world seems to be falling apart. Faith is not faith until it is tested and we have to fight for it.

The great gift to us as women is that we have each other. We are not designed to do life on our own, to struggle through, and to work out all our problems in isolation. Many times, I've sat with my friends when it feels like all hope is lost and been vulnerable about my own challenges and concerns. These are the times when having each other is what carries us through. We shouldn't hide under a rock, because we aren't meant to do this on our own.

So here I was, still trying for a baby, and it was time to buy an ovulation kit just to help things along—twenty quid well spent. Forget spontaneity—*we had to orchestrate our most intimate moments!*

Martin travelled a lot during this time, as things were very busy for the band. They had recently recorded their first album, *King of Fools*. Two of the songs, "Deeper" and "Promise," entered the UK charts in the top twenty and secured lots of exposure for Delirious? in Britain and across the Atlantic. This was followed by extensive tours and a real introduction to the American audience. The world was buzzing. The band were working hard and receiving numerous invitations to play. So what on earth was the use of this ovulation kit telling me, "Now is the time," when my hubby was somewhere in New Jersey?

Six months later, during the summer of 1996, I felt a little nauseous in the morning and gagged as I passed the fish counter at the local Sainsbury's grocery store. I stuffed a pregnancy test in between a packet of tea bags and a sliced loaf of bread and headed home.

I stood in the bathroom, ignoring the plastic stick that was sitting on top of the toilet. *I wouldn't look at it!* Not till it was ready. So I decided to sort the laundry until it was time for me to find out if my life was about to change. *No peeking! No peeking! Is it time yet? No, I'll wait a bit longer.*

I decided to turn it over. Where did I put the instructions? *Is there a line on the plastic stick?* I wondered. *What does that mean?*

If two lines appear, you are pregnant, the instructions read.

My eyes focused on the indicator and widened. I saw two lines. *Pregnant. I'm pregnant.*

I ran down the stairs and found Martin in the kitchen, raiding the fridge.

"Are you ready to be a dad?" I whispered.

Martin had no words, but then he was completely blown away and, like most blokes, felt that the success was his own—and he spent the

next week bragging about his manhood. Watching the lines mate-
rialise on the stick was enough for me to congratulate my estrogen
hormones.

Fashion magazines took a backseat, and I became obsessed with
"mum and baby" publications, with their pull-out charts showing
week-by-week growth. It was thrilling to check off the physical
symptoms as they aligned to the chart: "may need to empty bladder
more frequently"—oh yeah!

Soon the baby was the size of a kidney bean, and the time had
come for our first ultrasound at the hospital to see exactly what was
growing inside me. I had imagined this moment since I was a little
girl dreaming at my school desk: my pregnant self, floating into the
hospital with strings playing in the background and my husband
skipping down the hospital corridor, his hand in mine and love in
his eyes. Well, instead, we were late leaving because he was in the
studio finishing a song. He'd forgotten to shave and was still scrib-
bling down lyrics in the waiting room.

Idiot! I thought to myself. Sorry, but it's true. I know I should be
saying, "Praise God for such a great and godly man," but sometimes
I want to ram that microphone where the sun don't shine.

Food cravings came urgently and unpredictably.

We'd be lying in bed, ready for an undisturbed night's sleep (those
were the days!), when the memory of a McDonald's Quarter Pounder
would jump my taste buds like a thug in a back alley, and that ham-
burger would be the only remedy to get me to sleep. And Martin,
familiar with the pull of a bit of "late-night, post-gig fast food," would
dutifully demonstrate some agape love and silently depart the house
and disappear up the road in my little blue Ford Fiesta.

I'm sure Martin pulled his hair out—one minute it was toast and Marmite, the next definitely *not* toast and Marmite; one day two sugars in my tea, the next absolutely no sugar in my tea—in fact no tea at all. It didn't end there; one minute I cooked for the youth group, laughing and chatting as I do best, and the next I'd be exhausted without an ounce of energy or the inclination to do so much as plump up the cushions. Poor Martin tried to anticipate my feminine ways, but it's hard for the blokes to understand the idiosyncrasies that pregnancy brings with it.

The infamous morning sickness was so incessant, I remember passing an old lady in the village, wishing I could be her because I guessed she probably didn't feel sick. While working at the play centre, I'd feel faint and try my best to look after a room full of kids, when all I wanted to do was lie down. I'd glamorised being pregnant for so many years, thinking it would be everything I'd dreamed of, but here I was with my head down the toilet and a bag full of gingersnaps to satisfy my odd cravings. All-day sickness combined with a terrible urge to eat tomatoes and full-fat milk was a cocktail for disaster. Thankfully, at twenty-one weeks I began to feel "normal" again.

As my waistband expanded, so did my wardrobe. When I saw the indentation of my belt logo on my stomach, I decided to put the jeans away for a while—which was easier said than done. Fashion and maternity wear don't really go together, and, comfort or no comfort, I was loath to wear a pair of dungarees. So instead I continued with my wardrobe favourites (just in bigger sizes), including heels, which are a bit of a Smith trademark!

The due date came and went, leaving me more time to polish the taps and make the house look like a show home. The nesting phase had well and truly arrived—even the tins in the cupboard faced the right way, much to Martin's amusement.

On April Fools' Day 1997 the backaches and cramps accelerated. Before I knew it we were bombing over to the hospital, armed with new pyjamas, disposable pants, and a bag full of supplies. The big hospital bathtub relieved the pain, and Martin spurred me on from afar—as he was not the hands-on type—telling me I was doing really well. He'd sit down for a moment, then stand up for each contraction and repeat exactly the same words. My friend Helen England delivered her baby at the same time, so her poor husband, Paul, heard our screaming in stereo—and he confirmed that he heard every shriek!

9

WELCOME, ELLE-ANNA

Dear Mum
You're my only mum I've got. I love you so much and
with all my heart. Thank you for all that you have done.

With love from Elle xxx
—Elle (age 7)

Welcome, Elle-Anna Joyful.

At 6:53 a.m. on the second of April 1997—with the help of gas and air and Carol Patmoor, my lovely midwife—our beautiful daughter Elle-Anna Joyful Smith was born. What an amazing feeling! Holding new life in my arms was a precious moment despite being exhausted. She had dark blue eyes, brown hair that stuck to her face, and a tiny curled-up body. I felt sheer relief and joy that it was all over as I sat there reeling from the shock of the experience.

Our first child had arrived safely into the world—Martin felt ecstatic and extremely emotional at seeing his little baby girl, and I was proud to be living this moment with him and that he was the father of this brand-new life.

As Elle grew, so did her cheeks. When she learned to smile she didn't stop, her eyes danced, and her nose was a squishy button. She was my chirpy chipmunk, and I loved the new direction that life took us.

When Elle was just six weeks old, Delirious? played at Wembley Stadium for an event, and I was part of a dance team that accompanied the musicians. An audience of forty-five thousand people came out from all over Europe. As I waited in the wings onstage, I fed Elle, trying to bring both of us some relief. I jumped around onstage for a couple of hours in front of a sea of faces, trying to forget the discomfort, looking heavenward.

Elle bounced along during the first few months. She was round and happy, and surprisingly, she was an early walker. At ten months, she decided to get to her feet and exercise a little independence. At fifteen months, she showed off her new skills to her Auntie Suzi, who arrived on the doorstep with arms open, ready to entertain her niece.

Suzi brought sunshine into our house and, being a fellow dancer, was always ready to entertain us with a backflip or by doing the splits. She stayed with us while working at the headquarters of The Body Shop (not far from where we lived at the time), and our house was soon filled with heavenly smelling soaps and enough cocoa body butter to moisturise the whole street ... *for a year.*

One particular morning, as we bustled around getting ready for the day's events, Suzi became baffled as to the whereabouts of her car keys. Retracing her steps again and again, she grew increasingly anxious as the minutes ticked by. We turned the contents of the house upside down, but the missing keys were nowhere to be found. Suzi checked her handbag for the umpteenth time and was adamant that she had left them on her bed. Eventually, they were found in the rubbish bin, well and truly hidden at the bottom, in among the remnants of the previous night's beef casserole and a few jagged cans. Little Miss Innocent sat in her high chair, wearing a turquoise two-piece outfit, surveying the rising chaos and grinning like a chimp as she ate her cereal. Suzi, late for conducting her first tour of Body Shop HQ, dashed out the front door, irritated.

People sometimes ask me if we set out to have a large family. Martin was one of four, and I was one of five, so we were used to the joys of a big home, huddling together on road trips and squeezing onto the bench for supper. Having a much younger brother qualified me in early child care, and I carted Ben around on my hip as if I were his mother. My sisters had children before me, so I was often surrounded by the little darlings—and it was my passion, my academic training, and something in which I had confidence. Elle was an absolute peach with such an easygoing temperament, so, God willing, we were up for more.

Later on in Elle's first year we holidayed in Ilfracombe, a seaside town in North Devon, and managed, in among the thousands of other tourists, to find solitude in a camping field with Tim, Becca, and my mum and dad. Elle was promoted to a backpack, and we spent the time breathing in the fresh air and country smells. My mum cherished her new role as a grandma, while Grandpa spent most of the week in a deck chair with his head in a Billy Graham book.

Before the year concluded we saw our dear friends Matt and Beth Redman get hitched and my brother Jon marry his American

bride, Kristen, in a romantic Christmas candlelit ceremony in
Bethlehem—not the birthplace of Jesus, but *Bethlehem, Pennsylvania.*
Later that year, we took a whistle-stop tour around New York, went
ice-skating, and looked inside the FAO Schwarz toy store to conjure
up the Christmas spirit. We concluded our United States trip with a
flight to the Florida Keys, where we had just enough time to get the
sun on our faces before returning to the wind chill and plummeting
temperatures of the British winter.

For you created my inmost being;

    you knit me together in my mother's womb.

I praise you because I am fearfully and wonderfully made;

    your works are wonderful,

    I know that full well.

My frame was not hidden from you

    when I was made in the secret place.

    When I was woven together in the depths of the earth,

    your eyes saw my unformed body.

All the days ordained for me

    were written in your book

    before one of them came to be.

(Ps. 139:13–16)

10

PASS ME A BISCUIT ... QUICK!

Author or athlete, singer or shepherd, dentist or doctor, prophet or priest, minister or administrator, teacher or theologian, we thank God for this little life, and pray that he will bring pleasure, blessing, and relief to very many in the years to come.
—Love, Grandma and Grandpa Thatcher

No sooner had I chopped all my hair off and lost most of my baby weight, I found out I was pregnant again. It was the morning of August 5, 1998, and the wedding day of Dan and Nicola, some close friends of ours, so I hid a few gingersnaps in my beaded handbag just in case. However, with this baby, as I soon found out, the gingersnap craving subsided, and organic carrots became a must—in fact, I ate so many carrots, I actually turned orange. It was a lovely wedding, but to all those at table 7, apologies if I was a bit preoccupied. By the time we ate dessert, I had the name and the due date, and by the cutting of the cake, I had designed the nursery, too.

For the first seventeen weeks, the most ambitious act of the day was to make it downstairs onto the sofa and watch TV with Elle. Again, I felt like I was enduring a three-month sickness bug, but life had to carry on and Elle needed feeding, changing, and looking after. Martin had just begun to travel more intensely, which made being left at home pregnant and looking after a baby even more difficult. I always supported the vision of taking this music to the world, but that doesn't mean it was easy. I wanted Martin with me, and I spent many a lonely evening wishing he could be home.

Growing up, I wanted to be a mum who didn't get stressed out. So now I try to recognise the situations that I find difficult, and I do what I can to prevent them from getting to me. I make it my mission not to be grumpy. But when I do let it rip, it's Martin who is on the receiving end—everything becomes his fault—and out tumbles all the frustration, and I lump it all on his shoulders.

The countdown to the birth began and I began to feel like my skin wouldn't stretch any further. Where was Martin when I needed him?

Contractions began in earnest, but I was a few weeks away from the due date, so I put it down to phantom pains and acute Braxton Hicks. Martin was shooting a video for one of their songs, "Gravity," and I was in the middle of renovating the bedroom. We were still sleeping in the spare room at the time, and the baby wasn't due to arrive until it was all finished.

Sometimes things don't go according to plan. And my water breaking all over the airbed at ten that night was not something for which I'd planned. I phoned Martin in a mild panic and told him to get back as soon as possible. Within the hour my husband stood at the door wearing the costume from the video shoot and asking for my eye makeup remover before we went to the hospital. Half an hour later, I was lying on a bed nervously anticipating both the night ahead and the birth of our second child.

Suddenly, the midwife couldn't track the baby's heartbeat. In seconds everything changed. Before I knew it, nurses whisked me down to the operating theatre for an emergency C-section.

I remember the doctor shouting to his team, "This baby is not well, we need to get him out right now." As I lay there ready to be cut open, I felt a deep sense of urgency—I was desperate to get the baby out alive and healthy.

Martin waited outside the operating theatre, separated from me without any explanation. He waited for what felt like an eternity until the tension and silence were broken with the cry of a newborn.

Welcome, Noah Jasper James.

Noah joined the Smith family at 4:41 a.m. on April 17, 1999, weighing six pounds, eight ounces, and fully healthy despite our earlier concerns. Little was said as to why I had to have an emergency Caesarean. It had all been a bit of a blur, and the operation had left me feeling peculiar. Martin stayed with our little boy for three hours before I woke up from the operation, and he decided to name him Noah before I even knew that I had a son. Meanwhile my mum and sister Sarah went to our home to dry the airbed. Fortunately, Sarah is a nurse and was unperturbed by the experience!

We returned home four days later accompanied by presents and flowers. Over the next few weeks, countless cards were dropped through the letterbox to welcome the new kid on the block. But poor little Noah was back in the hospital a few weeks later with minor postbirth complications.

Martin had returned to America and was about to jump onstage when I called. I told him that Noah was getting ready to go under general anesthetic for an operation. I so badly wanted him by our son's bedside, but he was two thousand miles away, feeling helpless on the other end of the phone. Through the ups and downs of being a part of Delirious?, here we were in one of the lows—me watching over our son while Martin was stuck on the other side of the world. Thankfully, the operation was a success, and Noah came home the next day.

Every year, all band members and their families packed into tour buses for a three-week adventure round the United States. So just as we'd gotten Noah to sleep through the night, we started packing for the American tour—jet lag putting an end to the luxury of sleeping for a full eight hours.

The schedule was constant: West Virginia on Tuesday, Toronto on Wednesday, Chicago on Thursday, then on to Cherry Hills, Denver, and Colorado Springs. The weeks were full of gigs and baby earmuffs; Ben & Jerry's ice cream and Waffle House, the twenty-four-hour diner; hundreds of miles of American landscape; and a girls' day out in Hollywood (the boys can't have all the fun!). The final week took us to New Mexico and eventually home to the UK, with our cowboy hats on!

11

THEN THERE
WERE THREE

*Happiness is a perfume you cannot pour on others
without getting a few drops on yourself.*
—Ralph Waldo Emerson

It was December 31, 1999, the eve of a new century. We had a great party with local friends, and the old year went out with a bang: People flung glitter and streamers around the room, and there was lots of canoodling with loved ones.

In the early hours of the morning we took to our bed, only to be woken a few hours later. I love a new year, a brand-new unspoiled calendar, and resolutions that sound achievable but by February are nothing more than crazy ideas. A few days into January, I had a strong inclination that I was pregnant again—I was getting used to the signs. The test confirmed it, and we were thrilled with the news that our little family was growing.

Our excitement was short-lived.

A few weeks later, I started to bleed heavily as I stood in the kitchen making the children's supper. I knew that this wasn't normal blood loss. Utterly devastated and powerless to do anything, I knew that I was losing my baby. As I left the doctors' surgery, I felt an immense emptiness inside—I was left feeling shocked and numb. My sister Sarah, who had also experienced a miscarriage, provided immediate comfort—she knew, she understood, and she was my rock. I have a pretty levelheaded and optimistic approach to life and can usually pick myself up and move on, but this time I couldn't. There was a big empty hole that just wouldn't go away. The sparkle had vanished.

As the days and weeks progressed I still felt very pregnant, which was disconcerting. I decided to do another pregnancy test: *Maybe I hadn't lost the baby after all*, I thought. The test was positive, so I called the doctor only to be informed that high levels of estrogen were still prevalent in my system and would take a while to subside.

I accepted his diagnosis, and it brought closure to the intense sadness of the ordeal. Martin and I tried to remain positive, putting all our energy into raising our beautiful daughter and son. Elle celebrated her third birthday with a ballet party. Every photograph had her looking like she was having the worst time ever, stubbornly refusing to smile or pulling a stupid face in every snapshot. Noah's first birthday was footballs, tennis balls, and bouncy balls: an hour of ball heaven with celery sticks, his favourite snack.

As the weeks skipped by, my waist started to disappear, and the signs of pregnancy continued. Still confused, my mother's intuition made me take another pregnancy test. The little stick didn't need two minutes for the stripe to gleam back at me. Feeling a bit neurotic, I peeled open the second packet. Fixated on this window of hope, I watched as the blue line instantaneously surfaced.

I was pregnant, which didn't make sense. I'd already lost a baby. Then I realised that perhaps there had been two little lives growing inside me. Perplexed, excited, and bewildered, I phoned my mum and poured out all my questions and confusion.

Upon returning to the kitchen I found Elle and Noah enjoying the uninterrupted joys of free play. They had opened a tub of Vaseline and a box of cornflakes. Right, clothes off, time for a bath in the sink! I felt elation at the reality that I was still pregnant, but the realisation that I had lost a twin was heartbreaking. Heaven had called this tiny soul home.

Midway through my pregnancy we began contemplating a house move: somewhere with more space for more kids, room to entertain people from around the world, and a place to build a recording studio for Martin and the band so they could work closer to home. A beautiful Tudor manor house in the village centre had been on the market for a while. It was quintessentially English and far beyond our wildest dreams. Something inside us leaped at the idea. It had all the space we wanted and more. As my tummy grew, we watched and waited and prayed and let the dream grow; this big old house in the centre of the village seemed to have our name on it. But there was one small problem: We couldn't afford it.

Spring passed into summer, and the year moved into September, bringing us to the day of my grandfather's eightieth birthday celebration. I knew I was in labour before we left the house—I had woken up with stomach pains—but we didn't want to miss out on the party. By 4:00 p.m., the contractions grew stronger, so we organised child care for Elle and Noah and made our way to the hospital. I'd requested an epidural on my birth plan, but I was now eight centimeters dilated and the hard work was done. The epidural wasn't effective, and the pain was intense.

Just as I was about to grab the gas and air, the midwife took it away, saying, "Honey, you don't need this." But I did, I was in complete agony, so I did an unspeakable thing—I bit her!

Welcome, Indi-Anna Faithful.

Indi was born on September 9, 2000 at 11:06 p.m., weighing seven pounds, five ounces. Our second millennium present had arrived—and Indi was perfect. We quickly arranged to have Indi dedicated to God that same month, as we have done with all the children. We joined our wider church family in thanking God for another baby Smith and concluded the day with a walk along the seafront.

Meanwhile, the house move accelerated, and after weeks of deliberating and prayerful consideration we put in an offer that was accepted. Martin was deep in the studio recording *Audio Lessonover?*, so the heat was on in every area.

The house move got even more stressful in October. Two days before we exchanged contracts on the new house, our bank dropped out, and we were left with the choice of backing out or taking a huge risk. We chose the latter and exchanged contracts without a mortgage in place, which, upon looking back, was pure madness. It got worse when, the Friday before the Monday of completion, with all the construction workers scheduled to come out and renovate the house, our lender threatened to back out due to Martin's blood test results (needed for insurance purposes) being lost in the mail.

Luckily, someone found the blood test results on Monday morning, and so the insurance was approved and solicitors were notified; by lunchtime we had moved in with the help of friends and family.

The place needed total renovation, but we were here to stay. We told ourselves that God can do "immeasurably more than we can ask or imagine," and we felt at peace that this house would be our home. We had a deal, signed and sealed, and the keys were in our hands. Whoopee!

Renovations to the kitchen started to take shape, and soon we faced the joys of diggers, cement mixers, scaffolding, and plaster-board. The sound of drills and the radio blaring became the familiar wake-up call. Noah was in his element—a real-life "Bob the Builder." It was great entertainment for his impressionable little eyes, which would stare out the window for hours. As the old walls came down, our little family grew. Two labours of love in the making—one made of bricks and mortar and the other of flesh and bone. Newborn Indi played with a paintbrush for a toy and spent her first months wrapped in a dust sheet. It took ten weeks, four hundred cups of tea ("three sugars, luv"), and numerous packets of digestive biscuits. By the first sightings of the daffodils, our conservatory was erected, and new carpet had never smelled so good.

Alongside the house renovations, I grappled with the day-to-day craziness of caring for three children. Elle smiled loads, Noah was a nutcase, and Indi cried for three months straight, becoming really unsettled. Indi had developed a bout of colic, and it felt like the only thing that kept her happy was her swing. I'd feed her and she'd be fine, then she'd double up in pain, so I'd try and get a burp out—*no relief*. With two children in nappies and another one potty training, someone's bottom always needed changing or wiping. Usually, just as I stepped out the door, ready to leave the house, that fragrance would waft past me.

Right! Coat off, tights off, great, it's leaked up the back—*double joy.*

Am I ever going to get anywhere on time?

In a microsecond Elle had taken her shoes off, and Noah had escaped down the porch step. *Bump!* Loud wail. Big intake of breath, and then I'd lose it—having three kids three years old and younger was really hard work! At last, Indi, thankfully, accepted my milk without a cycle of pain, and things calmed down. Now, amazingly, she's the quiet one and doesn't easily show her emotions in public. She's very much a blend of Martin and me. She never complains, is very respectful and wise, and has a strong sense of right and wrong— she is our justice fighter.

The end of the year arrived, and the snow fell. Every shrub and flower hid beneath a picturesque white blanket. We had heaps of fun playing and building snowmen. It had been a hard, crazy year: We'd had another baby, moved, and the band had notched up 110 live shows around the world, which meant that Martin had been in and out, packing and unpacking all year long (thank goodness for Skype). I remember feeling like it was right to cut the cord on the year 2000, and time to start a new season.

So we entered 2001 with a huge New Year's Eve party to shake off the dust. Two hundred people helped us christen our new home as we celebrated life, love, and friendship.

Friend of angels.
Tall fair,
laughing eyes.
Strong heart.
Playful soul from my womb.
So tiny so quiet.
The angel came
for you.

In heaven's crib you grew,
her breasts your sweet milk,
her tender song your lullaby.
Have you swum an ocean?
Can you see the moon?

Do you paint
or write or sing?
Are your eyes of blue?

One day I will come.
We will kiss, touch, and laugh.
And walk a million miles
upon a sea of glass.

Chris Pringle, *Jesse Found in Heaven* (New Kensington, PA: Whitaker House, 2005), 11. Used with permission.

12

HOME SWEET HOME

Do not say to your neighbour,
"Come back later; I'll give it tomorrow"—
when you now have it with you.
—Proverbs 3:28

The new house became a gathering place for friends and family. Weddings, birthdays, and baby showers; book launches, BBQs, and youth events; New Year's Eve parties, pudding parties, and Valentine's parties; baptisms, thirtieths, fortieths, and even a fruit party for Jon's twenty-first. You name it, we celebrated it, and every mark on the carpet has a story to tell.

Some events weren't so successful, like the first firework night we had. The fireworks were fantastic, as was the huge hog roast. Unfortunately, we found out the next day that we weren't insured for letting off small explosives in our back garden with three hundred people present. Whoops, forgot about that detail! Martin was mentioned at the next parish council meeting for bringing danger to the various thatched roofs scattered around the village.

Allowing people to come into our home is really important to me. I want my home to be a place of eating, reading, praying, playing, dancing, and sleeping. Essentially, it's just a building of stone, but it's also a place to create memories.

Around this time, HopeHIV invited the band to Johannesburg to work with orphans, of whom 80 to 90 percent had been infected with HIV. The previous year Jon and Stew ran the London marathon to raise money and awareness for this amazing charity, so they jumped at the chance to be involved. The trip was life changing for the band, and it became the first of many visits to similar places.

Easter came around, and again we boarded the shiny buses for the American tour. The children squealed with delight when they heard that our travels would take us near Disneyland. The Disneyland visit was a highlight of the tour, and we all grew emotional when the closing ceremony started and fireworks filled the night sky. Stu G always cries at moments like this, and the *Fantasia* light show was no exception. These are the times when we all look around at each other, standing together as friends and family, grateful to God for being in this band and on this team, feeling like the most blessed people on the planet. These are the memories that we cherish.

Back home we started preparing for the day of Martin's sister's wedding. We were hosting the reception at our house, and a marquee was erected in our garden. Paul, Martin's eldest brother and merchandise guy for Delirious?, coordinated the whole event. Suzi scheduled the wedding on a day when there were no Delirious? shows so her older brother Martin was sure to be around. Giles, Suzi's husband-to-be, worked as a graphic designer for the band's record label, and it was a priority for it to be a "work-free" weekend—or so we thought!

Two months before the wedding day, the Delirious? manager, Tony Patoto, got a call from the management of Bon Jovi, asking if Delirious? would support them on their UK stadium tour. Wow! Even more amazing was the fact that the five shows would take place during the week leading up to the wedding, leaving the weekend free to attend the wedding! Of course Delirious? said yes.

But somehow life never goes to plan, does it?

The music industry and raising children are quite similar, really; you think you've got it sorted out when, *wham bam,* the phone rings and everything changes.

Two weeks before the wedding, the promoter called to say that the show at the Milton Keynes Bowl had been moved to the Saturday night. One small problem: That was the night of the wedding. To top it off, Martin was planning to sing at the wedding service. Big problem!

The boys called an emergency meeting to try and resolve an impossible situation, but with contracts signed and the Delirious? name on the publicity, there was no way out. Aha! Did someone mention a helicopter?

The Wedding Day—June 6, 2001
7:00 a.m.

Kids bounce on our bed, excited at being bridesmaids and page boy in the wedding. Martin was already tired from playing the night before at the Cardiff Millennium Stadium.

9:00 a.m.

The hairdresser arrives at our house and starts making fifteen ladies look beautiful. Martin strings his guitar and finishes the lyrics for the wedding song.

11:00 a.m.

Photographers from a bridal magazine arrive and start snapping photos of the bride. Rain clouds darken the sky. Martin disappears, and the band sound checks at the church.

12:00 p.m.

Suzi, the bride, arrives at church, looking radiant.

12:03 p.m.

Someone performs last-minute dress alterations. Martin finalises the lyrics on the back of the service program.

12:04 p.m.

The bridesmaids walk down the aisle.

12:06 p.m.

The bridesmaids are still walking down the aisle.

12:07 p.m.

Bridesmaids stand at the altar. Martin tucks in his shirt.

1:00 p.m.

Service finishes. The newly married couple leave for the reception in an open-top stretch Beetle. Martin and the band leave in the helicopter!

1:45 p.m.

More photos. The helicopter runs into a rainstorm and does emergency landing twenty minutes outside Milton Keynes, instead of backstage. The helicopter refuels but won't restart!

4:00 p.m.

Wedding guests wait to be served food. The band waits for helicopter to get fixed.

5:00 p.m.

Wedding speeches begin at the reception. The helicopter still won't work. A police escort turns up, and the boys are piled into the back of a police van and driven through Milton Keynes at 90 mph. Delirious? is due onstage at 5:20 p.m. for the biggest gig of their lives.

5:31 p.m.

Wedding speeches still going on. The band is eleven minutes late for the biggest gig of their lives, and they pass Bon Jovi as the police van screeches into the backstage area. With no time to change, they whip off wedding cravats and run onto the stage.

5:50 p.m.

Best man toasts the bridesmaids. The band leaves the stage after playing to eighty thousand people. The show rocked!

6:20 p.m.

The DJ turns on the music and gets the after-dinner dancing started. The band leaves Milton Keynes in a helicopter (now
fixed).

7:15 p.m.

Martin arrives back at the house and meets Great-Grandma
Gravenor in the driveway:

"Hello, sweet'art, did you enjoy the speeches?"

"Sorry, I've just got back," Martin says.

"From the loo, luv?"

8:00 p.m.

Suzi and Giles cut the cake as people shoot party poppers everywhere, and I get to slow dance with my man.

1:00 a.m.

The last few wedding guests leave.

2:00 a.m.

I clean the kitchen floor in bridesmaid's dress, with my mop and
bucket in hand. I look down at my grubby, bare, sore feet.

2:30 a.m.

Wash feet.

2:32 a.m.

Get into bed.

3:00 a.m.

Wake up to feed Indi.

13

A TOUGH YEAR

I expect to pass through life but once. If, therefore, there be any kindness I can show or any good thing I can do to any fellow being, let me do it now and not defer or neglect it as I shall not pass this way again.

—Author Unknown

Life is a tapestry of events and circumstances, some good, some bad. Some that bring joy to the soul and some that tear the heart out. Dark valleys sometimes appear without warning, and we have to deal with them as best we can.

The year 2002 took us into one of those valleys, one that shook the entire family. I was pregnant again. But little did we know that this was to be something completely different. When it was time for our twenty-week scan, Martin took the morning off to accompany me to the hospital. Like with the other pregnancies, I had overdone the water intake in the hope of a clearer picture and spent the whole time in the waiting room crossing my legs, desperate to visit the bathroom.

"Mr. and Mrs. Smith?" the sonographer says into the waiting room. "Would you like to follow me, please?"

I hop onto the bed and get my belly ready. I'm becoming a pro at this. The sonographer smears the gel on my tummy, and wow, there it is! I see a wriggling life on the screen. The sonographer takes all the head and spine measurements, and everything is fine.

I can't keep my eyes off my baby.

But as I look up, things seem different. The nurses keep looking at the area of the baby's heart. *What's going on?* Martin squeezes my hand. I feel sick. Is the baby okay? Is it healthy? What's going on? Doctors are striding in and out of the room, each of them looking at the screen. All looking at the baby—*our baby!*

I rearrange my clothes and sit up. The doctor goes to the door, closes it, and turns to face us.

"There's a problem with your baby's heart," he says. "One of the ventricles is misshapen, and it could lead to heart problems as your child grows. There's a chance your baby may not survive once it's been born."

The doctor continues speaking, but I can't respond. I feel numb. My world has collapsed around me.

The weeks and months that followed were like a bag of allsorts. Sometimes my own children saw me emotionally laid bare and would share tears with Mummy. Sometimes a huge faith rose inside me. Life went on with purpose and routine: driving to school, football matches, and gymnastic clubs, along with continuing house renovations. The hubbub of drills, vacuum cleaners, phones, and electronic toys tried to block out thoughts that might dwell on a dysfunctional heart. Yet it consumed my mind constantly. I never stopped thinking about it: the labour, the delivery, the sympathy cards, and even the funeral.

There were moments in the privacy of my home that I would stop what I was doing and get on my knees and pray—with the children, without the children, with whomever was with me at the time—*thanking God for the life inside me* and asking earnestly for a heart that would beat as it should.

After the twenty-week scan the doctor scheduled me for more checkups. We were referred by the obstetrician in West Sussex to the neonatal unit at St. Thomas' Hospital in London to discuss the diagnosis and condition of our unborn baby's heart. Mum looked after Indi and picked Elle and Noah up from school so Martin and I could travel together and listen to the consultant's prognosis without distraction.

That day we stood on the train station platform at Angmering and enjoyed a rare moment of time, just the two of us. The moment was reminiscent of the times we'd gone on a date to London; it gave us time to be a couple, to pray, to laugh, to chat, to plan; to sit in silence, holding hands and staring at the solitary cows grazing in the fields. As the landscape changed from green pastures to stark and ugly grey industrial sites, my heart raced, and waves of anxiety surfaced. I laid my hands over my child and silently prayed for good news.

Putting on a brave face, we sat in the hospital waiting room, flicking through out-of-date magazines without digesting any of the articles. The consultant arrived. He was younger than I'd expected and very knowledgeable and matter-of-fact. After a look at the scan images, he gave us an in-depth lesson about the muscle of the heart. Words like hypertrophic, dilated, and cardiomyopathy bounced around the room, but I was determined to digest all the information.

Next came the valves: pulmonary, tricuspid, mitral, and aortic. We were on a mission to learn what was happening inside our baby. Then he got a piece of paper from the printer and drew a diagram of the heart. On the reverse side he wrote cardiomyopathy, which could be one of three things: (1) a virus, (2) a biotem (whatever that was), (3) don't know. And that was it: stark, brief, and poignantly factual. And now we had a sketchy diagram representing three possibilities to an ineffective heart.

The pregnancy was so uncertain that we were left with lots of questions that couldn't be answered until the baby was born. So life continued. My bump grew bigger, the house continued on as busy as ever, and every unit of time seemed to have a purpose.

Martin travelled more and more as audiences rose from small groups of five hundred to stadiums of eighty thousand. Delirious? had invaded the United States, and popularity and demand across the Atlantic was growing fast. Early one Monday morning, five shiny gold discs arrived from America, certifying that five hundred thousand copies of the *Cutting Edge* album had been sold—an exciting achievement!

The band also began recording a CD for the South American market, which caused much amusement in the house—for weeks I was serenaded in broken Spanish while peeling the potatoes—Martin honestly thought he was some kind of Enrique Iglesias! It made the children giggle—*Daddy had finally lost the plot.* Then Martin went on the road again to South America with phonetic song sheets stuck to the floor with gaffer tape, just in case the Spanish lyrics got the better of him. Thankfully he was home by December, and on that night we received a phone call—one of those calls that changed our world.

My uncle John and auntie Jo and their four gorgeous daughters lived a stone's throw away from our house. John was my dad's younger brother and one of the leaders of our church. The first week in December, as we were all gearing up for Christmas, John flew to the Swiss Alps to visit a church there. It was a whirlwind visit, and we expected to hear news of the trip and see photos of snow-topped mountains.

On the evening of December 5 the phone rang:

"Uncle John died," my sister Becca said in a calm but eerie tone.

He had suffered a heart attack on the ski slopes, and they couldn't revive him. Nothing much else was said. Martin and I sat down and tried to absorb the devastating news. We felt completely numb and speechless.

That night the whole church gathered, bewildered and shocked at the news. The congregation wept and prayed, finding it hard to believe that this could happen to a forty-four-year-old father of four. At the end of the meeting, John's wife, Jo, and their daughters, Rachel, Naomi, Susannah, and Elisabeth, gathered in the middle of our community, devastated yet supported by a group of people that loved them dearly. It was an evening no one will forget.

John's death pulled the family together, closer and tighter than ever before. Everyone rallied around, offering help and comfort where they could, whether in the shape of a casserole dish, a hug, or just someone to sit and say very little. Jo flew out to Switzerland the next day, and the return flight home, with her beloved husband in a casket, was a journey that I can't even begin to imagine. We each tried to process the grief and the tragic loss of a very dear man. A week later we buried John at Worthing Crematorium. It was an intimate gathering of family and close friends. John's well-read, leather-bound Bible and his ski gloves lay on the top of his coffin instead of flowers. While the winter sun sat low and bright, we all clung together as best as we knew how. The young children in all their innocence and beauty gave relief to the intense grief, and the place was full of peace. Trying to comprehend such a tragedy, and knowing that heaven was now John's home, weighed heavily on our hearts.

Two days later a thanksgiving service was held at Littlehampton Senior School, where we held our Sunday services. The hall filled up with hundreds of friends paying their respects to a much-loved and humble man of the community—a selfless individual who lived to please others. Jo sat with her girls, exuding an inner strength that could only come from her heavenly Father. She held her youngest daughter's hand, while her eldest, Rachel, sang with Martin. It would be so easy to fall to pieces with a situation like hers, but from this devastating loss rose a mighty woman like the one described in Proverbs 31: "Clothed with strength and dignity; she can laugh at the days to come. She speaks with wisdom, and faithful instruction is on her tongue. She watches over the affairs of her household and does not eat the bread of idleness.... She sets about her work vigorously; her arms are strong for her task.... Her children arise and call her blessed" (vv. 25–27, 17, 28). Jo is indeed a wife of noble character and her husband's "crown."

The shows had to continue, and although no one was in the mood, it was the right thing to do. The crowds lifted the guys, and Martin began to sing "Mountains High" every night, which became a dedication to John. It's such a cliché to say that life goes on, but it does, although it's never the same. We missed John, and all these years later we still miss him. His absence created a huge void in our family.

Christmas was a week away, and the village lights glistened in the streets. We attended school and playgroup nativities, the house smelled of pine needles and cinnamon sticks, and everything looked festive. The events of the previous weeks left us all feeling flat, but the children, in their playfulness, helped to break the moments of silence. New Year's Day had always been spent at Jo and John's house, where John would slave away in the kitchen, cooking a hearty brunch for the entire family. This year, Martin and the band took on the mantle and cooked like Gordon Ramsay all morning. It was a quiet Christmas season that came and went without a fuss.

As we coped with losing John, the heart of our unborn child was still struggling and pressed on our minds. We became more determined than ever to stand in faith for this new life. A few days after John's death this letter arrived in the post from my in-laws:

To Dear Anna and Martin,

We shall be praying for you all the way over the next few days. We are praying the same prayer we did thirty-two years ago for "little Martin": "Lord breathe into his lungs and let him make a noise" except this prayer will be "inflate that ventricle." We pray that this little one will be born safely and soundly, and that the doctors and midwives will be efficient and be given wisdom as to the right course to take.

God knows all the emotions that you are and will be feeling, but he will be there right beside you as he promised.

With all our love
Mum and Dad Smith

Mountains High

Sorrow came to visit us today
Was the longest day, was the longest day
Sorrow came to steal our hope away
Only tears can tell
Of this holy hour

This mountain's high, too high for us
This mountain's high, too high for us
Too high

Sorrow came quicker than a fire
Was the longest day, was the loneliest day
I feel your hand, the warmth, your sweetest smile
But you slipped away, through the great divide

This mountain's high, too high for us
This mountain's high, too high for us

You know I'll make it through

Your ways are high, too high for us
Your ways are high, too high for us.

Martin Smith, "Mountains High," *World Service* © 2003 Curious? Music UK/Kingsway Music

14

OUR MIRACLE MAKER

The year 2003 began with heavy frost and plummeting temperatures. Wrapping Elle, Noah, and Indi up before the walk to school took extra time, and after dressing three children while standing in my coat, hat, scarf, and gloves, I often overheated. I only had a few weeks left until my due date, and recent scans didn't shed any further light on the condition of my baby's heart.

I used any spare time I had to glance over my prenatal notes. I wanted to be thoroughly prepared, so I read up on the high-tech equipment and procedures that might be involved, but honestly I had no idea what to expect from this birth. I'd done this three times before and yet remained apprehensive about the unknowns surrounding this pregnancy. I read chapters entitled "What happens if your baby dies?" And I let myself think about these things in the quiet spaces of my mind. I had decided how the funeral was to be, the style of coffin, the type of flowers. It's a strange thing to do, but it helped me to prepare myself. We'd been on a tour of the baby intensive-care unit, which was both moving and humbling. Tiny babies lay side by side, swaddled in bubble wrap to preserve heat, with electrodes placed on their chests to monitor heartbeat changes. Alarm pads lay under the incubator mattresses to signal any changes in breathing patterns. Machines and tubes dominated everything we saw, and yet, beyond all the medical paraphernalia, there were little miracles. We saw babies determined and strong in their quest for life, with brave and courageous parents who never stopped hoping.

Soon we would be joining these parents.

On February 4 we left Rustington for what we hoped would be our last visit to St. Thomas. It was two weeks before my due date, and I was going to have the baby induced—so the doctors could control the birth and be completely prepared for complications. My labour bag was packed, and my parents moved into our house in our absence to take care of the children.

With our mobile phones fully charged and a lot of prayer going before us, we drove into London, passing frantic shoppers itching to get a bargain on New Year's sales. We settled down for the night at the hospital, anxious for our baby, who would be born the next day. Amidst all the tension I had to laugh at my husband. The nurses provided him with a rickety old camp bed, which they'd set next to my big, comfortable bed. I could see he wanted to call up reception for a change of room.

We turned the lights out and prayed together.

I can't remember what was said, but I remember us holding each other in silence, both feeling anxious. Martin returned to his bed and snuggled down without even a blanket or a pillow. I chuckled to myself: This was the man I fell in love with, the father of my kids, not the guy that most people see standing onstage with a microphone.

The morning soon came, and Martin was a bit grumpy after a night with no pillow and because the tea lady wouldn't give him a spare cup of tea. We could see the houses of Parliament from our window, and London traffic was in full swing. I started my day by being hooked up to a drip and taking various medicines to jump-start the process.

Having this baby induced was a totally different experience, but from the moment things started "moving," everything went according to plan. Amidst all the fear and trepidation we both felt incredible peace and spent the whole delivery talking and reading the newspapers. The anesthetic had truly kicked in, and my baby was nearly here.

Welcome, Levi Jesse Jonson.

Six hours after the process began, our first blond child, Levi Jesse Jonson Smith, was born weighing eight pounds, three ounces, our biggest baby so far. On Tuesday, February 5, 2003, a new revelation of the Trinity came to me: God the Father, God the Son, and God the Epidural!

Of all my birth experiences so far, this was the best. In fact I would go so far as to say that I actually quite enjoyed it and felt a great sense of peace. We didn't feel fearful, because we knew that God was in control. There was a huge team of people in the room, all with their own unique job to do. Levi was immediately put on a breathing machine, wired up with sensors, and rushed down to intensive care to join the other babies fighting for their lives. I remember looking at him through the incubator, waiting for someone to tell me bad news. At first, I held back from allowing myself to bond with him because I wasn't sure how long we'd have together. He was purple, but, after hours of examinations, Levi was slowly taken from "alert" level down to "normal." And within days, amazingly, Levi was cleared to go home.

Yes, he was born with a strange-shaped heart, but he breathed well and for the most part was fit and healthy. The diagnosis was this: Levi had left ventricular noncompaction, something he would probably have for the rest of his life. But the doctors told us that he was to return home and get on with things as though he was normal!

So we left London with our tiny miracle, full of gratitude to the awesome staff, the ancillary, the surgeons, the midwives—*they are all heroes*. We dedicated Levi at church two weeks later on February 16. It was an emotional moment for me as friends and family gathered around us to pray and celebrate this precious life and answer to prayer. Within the space of two months we'd lost Uncle John but had been given Levi. John had a big heart for people, and though we didn't know it at the time, Levi carried the same love for others—so it was fitting to give him the middle name Jonson.

As the family multiplied, so did the laundry; as the meals grew bigger, so did the shopping bill; and as I looked upon my four children deep in sleep, so my heart expanded. I also learned many lessons. I guess I never know myself what I am good at until I try; I never know how much patience I have until it's tested. It's easy to get bogged down thinking about all the things I can't do, worrying about my inabilities and lack of experience or contemplating how skilled others are and not believing in myself. I once saw a great quote in a magazine and tore it out: "What you are is God's gift to you—what you do with yourself is your gift to God."

So what is my gift to God? My gift while I care for my children is to put every bit of every minute into being the best mother to them that I can be. God gave me these little treasures, the greatest gift I will ever receive, and with this treasure comes responsibility.

The band spent the majority of that year in the studio at our house. They tweaked and twiddled and grunted about music things—hooks and bridges and guitar tones—and kept their heads firmly planted in a book of music rhyme. I'd bump into them around the coffee machine, and I'd nod and smile. All the studio time meant they played only thirty-five gigs that year, not their usual ninety shows. In total they played to more than a million people, and between June and July they notched up 55,186 air miles each (that's a lot of frequent-flier miles to be used on holidays!).

The gigs stretched from the United States to Australia, and the boys' body clocks spun all over the place. The phone ringing in the middle of the night indicated their confusion about time zones: "Great to hear your voice, babe, but please call me when I'm awake!"

Jon managed to get back by the skin of his teeth for the birth of his second daughter, Xanthia, the fourteenth baby in the Delirious? daddy club. It's hard to believe, but some of the babies' births have been meticulously orchestrated to fit in with their daddies' schedules. In between the flying and the recording, the school runs and the lunch dates, the band finished off the next album. Martin and Stu G finalised the vocals. Everything became a little more hectic, and the guys got ready for an almighty show-and-tell—they'd worked hard and were excited about the album.

15

ALL BY MYSELF

Life can get lonely with Martin away and children to raise. It's hard when Daddy says good-bye, the door closes, and I'm left with children crying, wanting him back. On one occasion Indi looked at Martin and said, "You care more about the poor children than you do about me." That comment took a bit of follow-up time. Sometimes it's hard, especially when Martin and I dream together, and I'm the one left at home cutting toenails and fingernails on a Friday night as he's playing to crowds of thousands. Sometimes being alone means I need help from friends or family, especially when it comes to uninvited visitors.

One particular evening, not long after we'd moved into our new house, I had unexpected company. The children were asleep, and there I was at the kitchen table, writing letters, accompanied by a mug of hot chocolate and a packet of chocolates when suddenly I heard a distressing sound from the living room.

My heart leaped into my mouth as I tentatively crept across the floorboards to see what all the commotion was about. As I peeped through the door I saw a squirrel scampering and screaming around the room, clambering over the furniture faster than my brother-in-law Stew on his finest triathlon sprints. If you've never heard a squirrel screaming, imagine the high-pitched squeal of an overexcited three-year-old—*and it was so much worse than that!*

This was a job for the man of the house, but the man in question was somewhere in Tennessee. Fine help he was in my moment of crisis! It was up to me, but this was no spider in the bathtub! Taking a deep breath, I knew I had to get the French doors open to free the wild creature. As the squirrel completed his eighty-fifth lap, I sprinted into the room, head down and whimpering, and unbolted the door, my hands shaking in the process. I flung the doors wide open and vacated the room without so much as a "good night," shutting the adjacent doors behind me. God forbid that he should escape into the rest of the house.

His exit was urgent, thank goodness, and as I watched him disappear into the trees, my heart rate started to slow down. I shut the doors, surveying the claw holes in the sofa and the rodent droppings littering the floor. Scoffing down what I hoped were Revels without drawing breath, I reached for the phone and repeated the night's saga to the listening ear of my mother. The mice in the kitchen didn't seem so bad after that episode.

The infamous squirrel had made a quick exit, but he wasn't the only woodland visitor I had to face. One summer evening I had the bedroom window open and, as I often do when Martin is away, got myself into bed earlier than usual with a little bed picnic, my "read in a year Bible" book, and some other literature. No sooner had I finished my cheese on toast, when flying through the window toward me came a bat, flapping around the bedroom. I hid under the duvet, trembling with fear—"Help me, Lord, help me, Lord," I groaned pathetically. "What do I do?" With my head covered, I tried to think of a plan.

My hand snuck out of the duvet and scrabbled at the bedside table for the phone, knocking over a glass of water in the process. But the phone wasn't on the cradle where it should be, so I lay on my stomach and heaved my post-pregnant body onto the carpet, sliding like a worm, until I found it. Back in my tent I phoned my mum, begging her to come quickly—thank goodness she lives so near. The doorbell rang, and I belted out of the duvet, screaming and yelping as the bat careered around the room—*must shut the door.* My parents and brother Ben arrived. Ben was hard to identify with his hoodie zipped up—he held a torch and a fishing net, reveling at the prospect of the oncoming mission. Even though we never actually found the bat, we claimed a great victory that night; we were bat-free at last, and Ben was my hero. After shutting the bedroom window, I resumed my reading but still was wary of unwanted wildlife!

Another time I remember Indi drinking water from a flowerpot and getting violently sick. On two separate occasions she hit her head on the coffee table, and her head had to be "glued" back together. Elle burnt her arm on the boiling water from one of the baby bottles and another time drank a bottle of children's medicine unsupervised (how much I will never know!). I felt like the worst mother in the world.

Why do calamities happen when you are on your own?

Over the years I've realised the necessity of keeping going when the traveller returns. He's exhausted, I'm exhausted, but the children never seem to be. The family roles are often thrown up in the air and who knows where they might land, so it's good to keep a practical head. I've found it best to not switch off when I hear the key in the door after he returns from a ten-day tour. Mind you, I'll never turn down a visit to the local beauticians. Maybe this is why I have point-blank refused to have the hairdresser come to the house—a cup of tea and a magazine in a salon is an outing worth savouring.

To My Dear Sweet Indi

I just want to kiss you and squeeze you!
You have sunshine in you and I love you SO much.
You bring joy to so many people,
And I miss you so much!

—Love, Daddy

16

FLIGHT 378

I'll see you when I get there, shining like the sun.

In April of 2005, the Smith household was a hive of activity. Birthdays are a big feature of this month, and it seems that before the balloons deflate and someone eats the last of the cake remnants, we're already lighting more candles and doing it all over again. To add to the celebrations, the Easter Bunny always pays a visit, and chocolate starts to take over the shelves.

This April also began our regular American tour, but this time things weren't as fun as usual. We spent that whole trip on the road living with a great sadness.

I had the suitcases out, with an added one for Levi, who was to make his maiden voyage at the tender age of two. A few weeks earlier I had discovered that I was pregnant with our fifth baby, and at seven weeks I felt the familiar exhaustion creeping up on me, sapping my energy.

It was a relief when bedtime finally arrived the day before our departure. Keen to get the children to sleep so I could start packing, I made story time briefer than usual (although when they can read for themselves they know when I'm paraphrasing!). Then, just when I thought it was time to say good night: "Mum, can you read a Bible story?" I should've been celebrating with the angels that my dear little lambs wanted to know Jesus more, but I wasn't going to get suckered! It's probable that the kids were trying to eke out more time before they had to go to sleep. I gave in and read the story of Jesus healing the blind man at a speed that had him sprinting to cleanse his eyes in the Pool of Siloam.

I closed the book, switched the lights off, and said, "Good night and God bless, child one, two, three, and four. I *don't* want to hear you till the morning!" Then I gathered my to-do list, pondering a hundred and one jobs floating around my head. Ready for a productive evening, I set about packing.

I had been experiencing stomach cramps all evening and ignored them, but as I sorted out a month's supply of clothes into seven suitcases, the cramps stopped me in my tracks. I thought my body was telling me to stop and take a breather.

Throughout the night I started to bleed, which was accompanied by more pain, which got progressively worse as the early-morning sun peered through the curtains. We had an early start, and the children, with the help of Martin and Elle, got themselves dressed. A cereal bar sufficed for breakfast, which meant no mess and no car sickness.

By now my bleeding had grown heavy, and I suspected the worst. Two decisions lay on the table: First, cancel the trip and go see the doctor; or second, continue on with the trip and see a doctor in America.

In my mind, there was no decision to make. Not going would have devastated the entire family—excitable children looking forward to seeing their daddy onstage and spending a month on a tour bus with their cousins. I'm a fairly practical, levelheaded person, so I just went into autopilot, zipped up the cases, and headed downstairs. The journey to the airport lasted an eternity; I stayed quiet and tried to keep as still as possible, wondering how the day would unfold.

We arrived at Heathrow Airport, and I left the children with Martin and went straight to the ladies' bathroom. I felt horrible, and the bleeding had gotten heavier.

I wasn't sure I could walk another step, let alone face a transatlantic flight. But I had no choice. I told myself that I just needed to steady my head and my heart—I knew I could do this. I had an incredible sense of peace, and I knew that God would help me. *He's helped me before; I just need to trust Him to help me now.*

"Right, kids, everyone all right? Levi, darling, let me wipe your sticky fingers. Indi, your blanket must be around here somewhere, let's look in your bag."

We boarded the plane, and the discomfort became intense. Every now and then, a new wave of pain hit me. I bled so much I was afraid to even leave my seat. Levi sat between a tall businessman and me. The man wasn't happy to be travelling next to a toddler, and he made that perfectly clear to the flight attendant. He huffed and puffed at any movement Levi made, and we hadn't even left the runway yet. I knew it would be a long flight.

I sat motionless and fearful, powerless to do anything as this little life inside left me. Martin sat behind me, helpless with one child either side of him, but he constantly looked my way, embracing me from a distance. He was painfully aware of the magnitude of the situation but unable to rescue me.

Time stood still. Tears flowed silently. My heart broke.

Finally, we landed. I thanked God that the horrific journey ended. Martin and I waited until every passenger exited the aircraft. I stood to my feet, and he wrapped his sweater around my waist and hid the bloodstained seat cover as he slowly helped me off the aircraft.

Itineraries were tight and busy, and each day took us to a new venue with new schedules to follow. The show went on, and Delirious? didn't disappoint. Fans came by the thousands, ready to rock and thirsty for a touch of heaven.

Throughout the tour, I felt empty and heartbroken, grieving for my baby and trying to deal with such a huge loss. I glimpsed moments of Martin's pain behind the microphone, moments when he was bare and vulnerable, and yet somehow we both found the strength to push through. As soon as one concert ended, we were back on the bus, eating pizza and rolling into our bunks. We travelled through the night, across the vast American terrain, and woke ready for the hustle and bustle of the new day.

One morning, Martin grabbed my hand, having arranged for Becca and Sarah to mind the children, and he took me to a quiet place. It was day four, and we hadn't had a minute to be alone. It was a precious moment.

Wrapped in each other's arms, we wept for the loss of our child. Once the tears flowed they didn't stop, and the rest of the concerts featured an extremely emotional lead singer doing his best to get through each set. One night the boys came offstage to find Martin slumped in Jon's arms, sobbing uncontrollably—he'd been able to stay strong up until then, but the pain of this experience made him raw and tender. Martin has an unusual ability to feel things very deeply, but I had never seen him *so* deeply affected by anything before. His friends and family were there to carry him through that tour. All we wanted to do was go home, but it wasn't possible.

The tour continued. We went through many boxes of tissues, and we hid sore, puffy eyes under our sunglasses. Each day started with breakfast and morning activities, be it a park, a walk, or a town visit. We spent afternoons at a swimming pool for games of water basketball or underwater acrobatics. Girlie shrieks could be heard from Elle, Rosie, Abi, Kaitlyn, and Eden as they enjoyed the treat of a warm afternoon shower. The younger children spent their time bobbing around the water with enough inflatables to keep them well and truly afloat.

The last stop of the tour was in Nashville, and the band was in for a treat. They'd won a prestigious music award for their involvement in a soundtrack record for the Chronicles of Narnia film. This celebration concluded an emotional time with more tears, but this time we cried tears of joy. Touching down at Heathrow Airport wrapped up another epic tour, with lots of memories and photographs to put into albums. But it had also been an extremely sad time for us as a family.

We had said good-bye to a tiny soul and experienced deep heart-ache and sorrow. However, we had also known God's comfort—our baby was on the birth register of heaven.

When we drove onto the M25, we found it jammed with cars. As we drove home, my mind escaped to the start of a new school term and how much laundry detergent I needed for seven suitcases full of clothing. Had I polished the children's shoes? I mustn't forget school-trip money and the reading journals that needed to be signed. My head filled up with the domestic necessities needed to get life in some sort of order.

I'll See You

> I'll see you when I get there,
> Shining like the sun.
> I'll see you when I get there,
> Into your arms I'll run.
>
> I see you when the wind blows,
> Running without fear,
> Born to rest in your Father's arms,
> Your joy has dried the tears.
>
> I'll see you when I get there,
> When my life's complete,
> Will you take me to Jesus' feet?
> Hand in hand we'll sing.
>
> We're gonna sing for you.

Martin Smith, "I'll See You," *The Mission Bell* © 2005 Curious? Music UK/Kingsway Music

"God has been good to us. Seeing your kids peek through the half light of a concert and then joining us onstage is something special."—Martin

17

EXPANDING WAISTLINE

It's not the going away that gets me into
trouble, it's the coming home!
—Martin

Time heals, and life continued at a cracking pace. We squeezed in
some family time with our friends the Hamiltons, and upon returning from this holiday, we discovered that I was pregnant again. Due
to the miscarriage, I felt more anxious through my first trimester.

Soon, though, the boys were back in the States, in Seattle for an
outreach concert for street kids. The show was for kids who loved
skating, BMX bikes, and basketball. I remember Martin trying to
explain over the webcam how their show opened with a boy on his
BMX bike somersaulting through the air over Stew's drum kit. Noah
and Levi were very impressed!

Before the year was out the guys were back in Johannesburg,
South Africa, but this time with a very important guest. Brian Ball,
the head teacher of one of our local primary schools, went to be

with the band and develop a connection with the HopeHIV project. Brian was interested in getting his school involved in understanding how the majority of African children lived. Tim Jupp, keyboard player of Delirious?, was about to turn forty and decided to throw a party for all the street kids in Durban. They celebrated in style, not at the Ritz Hotel, but with a big tub of ice cream, among children who had no shoes.

The year 2005 had barely begun when Martin flew to India. The Christmas decorations were well and truly packed away, and, apart from a few seasonal leftovers, we got into the swing of a new year. The children had just gone back to school when Martin's suitcase was out, packed, and ready to go. He was especially excited about this trip to Hyderabad, India, because they were going to work with Joyce Meyer, an inspirational speaker and pioneering evangelist.

So both of us were back at work—one performing to crowds of over four hundred thousand and the other wiping bottoms and keeping Pampers in business.

And here's where it happens: the phone call that changes things for Martin, and for us.

The phone rings just as I'm straining the potatoes and promising the waiting tribe that supper's nearly ready.

"Indi, get back to the table.... Noah, try not to spill the water, my love.... Elle, can you encourage Levi not to arch his back in the high chair?"

Chaos.

I'm feeling slightly nauseous, and I wish the pregnancy hormones would take mealtimes into consideration—it's far too inconvenient for me to have my head down over the toilet right now. I hear ringing from the other room.

I rush to pick up the phone.

"*Helloooo,* Anna here."

"Hi, love, how are you?" Martin says.

"Yeah, good … general supper-time craziness, but we're all fine. How's your day been? What've you been up to?"

As he replies, I sense something different in Martin's voice tonight. I don't know, he seems bothered or troubled … *just different.* But there's no time to chat.

"Can't you phone in a couple of hours?" I ask him.

"Probably not," he replies. Later I guess that he'll be onstage or fast asleep in his hotel, I don't know, I get confused with the time zones. He starts to talk about everything he's experienced in India and his heart's caving in at the poverty he's seeing.

What can I say?

"Sorry, honey, must be awful," I say. "Right, got to go, the broccoli's disintegrating."

My words sound pathetic. And I can't quite hear him anyway as the line is breaking up.

"Bye, I'll call again soon, I love you."

What horrible timing! As Martin wrestles with the impact of this great poverty he's seeing and experiencing, I'm here trying to hold down the fort. He's getting "all emotional" about someone else's kids but all I can think of in that moment is how I need him here. Our children miss their daddy.

But every trip to India seems to ratchet up the intensity inside Martin—something's breaking his heart: He's moved, challenged, and provoked by everything around him there. *What's God saying? What's shifting?* Martin's seen poverty before, but this is something else altogether. It's another telephone call we'll have to resume later when the kids are in bed and my head's clearer.

The thing is, I want him in the kitchen with me now, pouring out his heart to me, like a proper married couple going on this journey of discovery *together*.

Not tonight though. He's somewhere in India, and I'm watching *Pop Idol* on TV.

But little did I know in the midst of the chaos of that night, God was working my husband's heart for a special purpose that would only be fully revealed later.

Imagine a typically rural scene in England: birds singing, bees humming, and rambling meadows, all under the backdrop of an ancient castle. What made this evening even more perfect was that this was our dinner venue, and my parents watched the children—bliss! Quality time with my man is high on our priority list when he's home. In addition, our dearest Aussie friends, Mark and Darlene Zschech, who were staying at our house on the airbed, joined us. Both couples had tight schedules that were difficult to synchronise. So the fact that I was forty weeks pregnant and ready to pop wasn't going to stop me from a night of intellectual and inspirational conversation, or so I thought.

Getting dressed for the occasion didn't consume too much time as my choice was limited to two pairs of trousers or a dress that Elle disapproved of—she remarked on it being far too short. However, I took her advice and opted for the sensible black trousers, jazzing them up with leopard-print shoes with satin red heels, far too high for my third trimester, but this was my fifth pregnancy, and the rules were well and truly relaxed. I wore scarlet lipstick to match and a squirt of perfume to take the attention away from my puffy fingers and swollen ankles.

As we got in the car we chatted and giggled, enjoying some time alone. We drove through the castle gates, taking in the ambience of the historical ruins, and proud daffodils greeted us as we proceeded up the driveway. The restaurant didn't disappoint, and the notes from the grand piano bounced into every crevice of the old stone walls while we ate.

I had felt mild contractions all day but kept this fact to myself. I felt sure they would pass. Halfway through my sun-blush tomato, caramelised onion, and feta tart I was led to believe that this *was* the real deal, so I excused myself from the table and headed to the ladies room. The helpful French waiter pointed me in the right direction, and I gingerly climbed the steps to my destination, hoping that I wouldn't give birth on the way! As I leaned over the sink and took a few deep breaths I realised we would have to skip dessert, which grieved me ever so slightly as I was looking forward to the sweet chocolate fudge pudding—*my favourite*. With my first or second baby I may have given in to the temptation, but I didn't want to take any chances.

Martin had already paid the bill and apologised profusely as we left our guests. I wondered if it was bad etiquette to ask to put the fudge cake in a doggie bag. Maybe Darlene could slip it in her hand-bag and let me enjoy it after I had done a hard night's work!

The hilly, winding valleys of the South Downs are a great local treasure but a pain in the neck when you're trying to get somewhere fast. However, when we reached the hospital they told us to head home for a good night's sleep, as things seemed to have slowed down. A good night's sleep it was not, for us or for the Zschechs, as the airbed had deflated! These poor, lovely people had come to stay with us and ended up on a punctured bed, hugging the floor-boards. At the crack of dawn I knew I was in established labour, so we headed back to the hospital. My water broke in the car park at 7:45 a.m. At 8:13 a.m., less than thirty minutes later, our fifth child arrived.

Welcome, Ruby-Anna Peaceful.

Our baby girl was born on Saturday, April 23, 2005 at seven pounds, one ounce, to the number-one tunes of Natasha Bedingfield and with Manchester United at the top of the English Premiere League. Elle, Noah, Indi, and Levi all huddled round the bed to catch a glimpse of their new sister, while their grandparents cradled their thirteenth grandchild. Seeing Darlene and her beautiful smile and an arrangement of flowers bigger than herself was a very welcome sight. Next to sneak in behind the curtains were Stew and Sarah, Abi, and Jemimah, just as Jon, Kristen, Pip, Karen, Nana, and Grandad were leaving. They all stood like sardines, whispering behind the curtain so that the nursing staff didn't know we were bending the allowed number of visitors.

At 7:00 p.m. on the same evening the doctor discharged us from the hospital, just in time for another episode of *Pop Idol*. We arrived at church the next day with our daughter in our arms and had her dedicated on the spot. After church, we entertained 110 people at our house for lunch, with everyone bringing a dish to share.

Tracey, my midwife, arrived in the afternoon for her daily rounds and was forced to search the house and garden for the newborn and her mother. With her weighing scales in one arm and postnatal notes in the other, she anxiously scanned the crowd. Midwives freak out if you have more than ten guests (because they can overstimulate the baby). Needless to say, when she eventually found me I got a stern talking-to. I would like to tell you that I had an early night, but this simply wasn't true.

I was having way too much fun.

18

LIFE IS FOR LIVING

*Playing music for a living is fantastic, but playing music
with your kids on the road is even more amazing.*

—Martin

Just in case you weren't yet aware, I love a full house.

I love everyone getting involved: someone stripping a chicken,
another friend putting the kettle on, a friend of a friend grating some
cheese, and a friend of a friend of a friend quartering strawberries!
The more the merrier.

I've moved on from the days when I'd strive to get everything
done before opening the door to greet the visitors. With little ones,
I'm up for receiving any help I can get—the kitchen is situated in a
way that any newcomer can find the food platters if they look hard
enough. I love to open up our home, and we've hosted many an
impromptu picnic in the garden. On a hot summer's day Martin
can't resist the urge to grab the microphone at the end of a Sunday
service and invite the whole church to join us for lunch. Not all three

hundred members turn up at our house, but often many do. BYOE (bring your own everything), and you're done—and suddenly it's an afternoon of catching up with your mates. All are welcome, but please don't be offended if you're thrown a towel or a pair of barbecue tongs at some point during the afternoon.

When I was a little girl I used to play "paper people" with my sisters, Becca and Sarah. We would act out scenarios where our dollies, made out of old magazines, would go to each other's houses, knocking on the door for lunch. Maybe during one of our role plays my dolly was rejected for tea by an unkind "paper neighbour," which might explain some deep-rooted pact that I have with myself to not intentionally exclude anyone.

The year gathered momentum as the band enlarged their territory. India, Asia, Africa, and Australia were now locked into the yearly schedule, in addition to the European tour, trips to America, and time spent recording new music. Sometimes I'm not sure if Martin knew what hemisphere or time zone he was in. The families of the band accompanied the boys when possible, but as you can imagine, with five wives and fifteen children among us, it was quite an expensive feat.

By the time Ruby reached her first birthday she had travelled to Singapore, Thailand, Tenerife, America, and Australia. It was vastly different from the half an hour car journey to New Forest that I was accustomed to as a child. Ruby, however, wasn't that impressed with the variety of cuisine. Try as I might to introduce her to avocado or butternut squash—or anything else, for that matter—she would spit it out in protest; it was a very challenging and frustrating few months.

When Ruby was four months old we travelled to see our friends in Thailand, and we stopped off at Singapore for the band to play an event. While Martin was at a press conference, I stayed at the hotel room, getting the five children ready to explore the shops on Orchard Road. Hotel-room doors seem to be made of the heaviest wood possible, as Levi, our inquisitive two-year-old, found out. While I was searching for a lost sandal he somehow managed to get his index finger trapped in the door hinge. Soundproofing or no soundproofing, the screams could probably be heard in the next hotel. I grabbed him, realising that his finger was hanging by threads, called my sister Becca to look after the others, and ran with Levi onto the streets of Singapore, shouting, "Hospital! Someone tell me where a hospital is!"

Thankfully the hospital was nearby, and I ran in, sweating in the humidity, along the pristine white corridors. The hand surgeon was so professional and efficient, and the whole staff mirrored his competence. He gave Levi a general anesthetic and operated that afternoon. Meanwhile, back at the hotel, Becca juggled eight children and tried to locate Martin. At the time, Ruby was still a tiny baby screaming to be fed.

Finally, a shocked Martin returned, grabbed Ruby, and ran to the hospital. A few hours and a very successful operation later, we raced out of the hospital as Martin had missed the sound check for the show. He had just enough time to put his stage clothes on and get out to the microphone. My little boy and I skipped the gig and instead ordered a round of Nutella sandwiches (for Levi) and some local sushi (for me). Keeping Levi's hand out of water for the rest of the trip was a nightmare—and he was left watching the rest of the children jump into swimming pools while he perched on the edge.

Things took a very global turn for Delirious?, and the lineup for that spring was Sydney, Singapore, and the United States. We accompanied the guys for our sixth tour and got to catch up with our American friends. Sometimes we see these people more than aunts and uncles in our homeland. It was the first tour in fourteen years for which Stew didn't join us, as he was training for a triathlon—finishing an impressive third—but we missed him and his family. It was again another incredible family adventure from New York to Nashville, clocking up over three thousand miles.

In the summer, Martin and Stu G took their guitars to Rwanda to a national stadium to get help with the 100 Days of Hope project inspired by Mark Zschech. Seeing twenty to thirty thousand people singing along to "Majesty" and other Delirious? songs was worth every heavy-eyelid moment for them.

It had been ten years since the band had gone full-time. Who would have thought that the yearly schedule could easily include trips to India, Malaysia, Australia, Indonesia, Africa, Ukraine, Croatia, Germany, and Switzerland? Sometimes it took days of travel just to play a forty-minute set. Some evenings, Martin would call just as the tour bus was leaving the mountains of Romania, and then I'd hear his keys in the door while we were all having our cornflakes the next morning. Our very organised breakfast time would suddenly turn into mayhem as all the children rushed to the front door, screaming, hugging, kissing, and wiping bits of breakfast cereal all over Martin's face. Rock 'n' roll, honey!

19

CREATIVITY AND COMPASSION

Return from overseas trips brought new waves of creativity out of Martin. As well as writing Delirious? songs, he also wrote with many other musicians.

In June, Michael W. Smith came to the house with his charisma and contagious laughter. He danced with the children and listened to their adventures with wide eyes, entering into their world of make-believe. Being a father of five children himself, he fit right in. In July, Matt Redman joined us, which thrilled the children as he also brought his wife, Beth, and their children, Maisey, Noah, and Rocco. I love how, even when the guys are in the studio, they still make time to come out and kick the ball around with the boys or watch the children dance.

The lovely Darlene came over next, chatting over a smoothie, peeling carrots, helping Levi tie his football boots, and feeding Ruby her banana and custard. She's become a beautiful friend over the years and has inspired me to be the woman God has created me to be. One minute we'll be laughing our heads off, talking about cooking disasters, and the next we'll be crying over the orphaned children we've met on our travels. Darlene is a devoted wife and wonderful mum to three gorgeous girls. A lot of people would imagine that her life is always full of roses, but here is a woman who has walked a hard road and continually paid the price for being so committed to the unique calling on her life.

The "grandfather of worship," Mr. Graham Kendrick, visits frequently, always arriving ready to inspire and create. You can almost set your watch by Graham's arrival—he has a meticulous work ethic and fierce attention to detail. For many musicians, starting in the studio at 10:00 a.m. means getting going by elevenish; not Graham. At 9:59 there he is, ready with pen and paper and notebooks full of lyrics to unleash. Martin was fourteen years old when he first heard Graham sing at a Christian event in Skegness, so it was an honour for him to have this amazing lyricist with him at pivotal points on the journey.

Tim Hughes, whom we affectionately call "Mr. England," came around and was, at the time, preparing to become a daddy. Tim and Rachel and their two children, Phoebe and Simeon, join the long list of people who have slept on the sofa bed, staying up late talking about football, parenting, and the hard questions about life. You would chuckle seeing Martin and Tim trying to put fresh sheets on the bed, twittering on about football player Cristiano Ronaldo and Avalon guitars. Rachel is cleverer than all three of us put together, and I learn so much in her company.

Chris Tomlin visited soon after, and his smile always lit up the room. I've made it my personal mission to find an English wife for Chris, but so far have failed miserably! He's always full of energy, not one to sit still for long. Another American visitor was Steven Curtis Chapman, a guitar-playing, songwriting, and singing genius.

Over the years, each artist had been invited to take part in an event called "Worship Explosion" at our local church. This was a time for the church to engage in an extended evening of praise and worship with some of the best worship leaders of our time. In this season something else began stirring inside Martin, though we were unsure of exactly what it was.

The boys returned to the States in June 2006. They travelled to America with the regularity of a worker commuting by train into London. But once they were back on board the aircraft, they had to think about the garden gate that needed fixing, or replacing the gold-fish that had died while Daddy was away. Martin's job has never been the average nine to five. And as hard as it is when I'm on my own, when Daddy can do the school run or maybe help out on a school trip—he always will—this helps maintain a sense of normality.

After a busy summer we were looking forward to going on holiday. The night before we left, as we sat on the luggage, Martin entered a new dream into his journal: the idea of getting a whole load of songwriters together to come up with some great anthems for the church. All these recent months of writing with Michael, Matt, Darlene, Graham, and Tim started him thinking about something bigger, perhaps spending a week together to write.

So with some vague ideas on paper and luggage by the front door, we left it at that, just thinking, dreaming, and letting this vision germinate. However, after a troubled night's sleep Martin woke with India on his mind and lots of thoughts swimming round his head. He couldn't escape his desire to bring these songwriters together to do something for the people he'd met in India. He wanted to do a project in which *all* the profits would be given away—which was a challenge within the traditional publishing system.

There had to be a new way, a new way of sending the songwriters' royalties directly to the humanitarian projects on the ground, bypassing the music industry. We knew we needed a bright idea. With these thoughts banging around in our heads, we focused on getting the kids in the car—*we had a flight to catch*.

The holiday was just what we needed, time to enjoy being a family, with all the dramas and highlights that vacations offer. We tried to keep things as simple as possible with so many little people. That meant lots of swimming, with someone perfecting a new dive bomb, while the youngest learned to swim with no armbands.

Martin and I buzzed with the idea of getting all these artists together to write for a bigger cause. Was it possible to manage it with everyone's crazy itineraries? How would each artist respond? Lots of questions with no answers—but the more we talked, the more amazing it sounded; maybe even history making.

Martin called Matt Redman in early September and told him about an idea of a songwriters' retreat that would generate new music. Martin talked about the vision of how giving the money away could model something new and radical. Thirty seconds into the conversation Matt jumped all over it—*he loved the idea*. The reactions were similar to those of the other writers: Darlene Zschech, Michael W. Smith, Tim Hughes, Steven Curtis Chapman, Israel Houghton, Andy Park, Chris Tomlin, Paul Baloche, Stu G, and Graham Kendrick all jumped on board.

Could this be something that would make God smile?

I was excited too, as the project became something to which I felt personally connected. For so many years the band had always felt like Martin's thing, and my role was simply to support him. But I was thriving on this new project and the greater purpose. Every day a new piece of the project fit the puzzle, and Martin and I were in this together. I would never call myself a charity worker or a singer, but I was about to embrace a bigger role as this dream became reality. The high chair still needed wiping a hundred times a day, but I started to feel passionate about being a kind of mum to those who had nothing. I felt a new call to work beyond my own limitations and comfort zone.

A few weeks later Paul, my brother-in-law, and Martin took a long journey through the night to Essex to be at the funeral of their grandmother. That drive from Newport to Woodford Green ignited some lengthy discussions. Martin talked about his idea for helping those he'd seen living in extreme poverty in India, and gathering all these songwriters to be a voice for change. Martin asked Paul if he'd be able to help, and Paul accepted.

Back at home for Christmas—and it was Friday night, usually the time that Martin would be warming up his voice and getting ready before a show. Tonight there were no crowds and no venue, just a sofa date with me. He felt tired, happy, and sad; his throat felt like sandpaper, and he thought he had broken a toe leaping off Tim Jupp's keyboard (zero sympathy there, my love!), but he was proud of the fall European tour of the last six weeks. For me Christmas started in the best possible way: with my husband, a bowl of chocolates, a foot massage, and the chance to fall asleep in each other's arms.

20

A HELPING HAND

Another tour, another crowd, another continent, another plane ride. So why does it feel like my heart has been pulled out, turned around, and put back a different way around? Why do I feel like life is never going to be the same again?
—Martin, January 2007

The intensity of Martin's travel increased in 2007, and it became apparent that I needed some help. The band had scheduled a lineup of more international concerts, and I began to feel slightly nervous about the logistics of taking so many small children on a long journey. In the past my band "sisters" had been amazing, providing hands-on help, but now I was beginning to feel outnumbered.

The incident with Levi's finger was a wake-up call to take action—one can only see so much, and at the end of the day my children's safety is my number-one priority.

One day the doorbell rang and in walked a sunny, smiley young lady called Eszter from Hungary. Help had arrived! Good friends who knew our predicament recommended Eszter to us as an au pair. She came to stay for the week, and we clicked straightaway. She was natural and friendly, outgoing and cheerful, which checked my first point of criteria—and the job was hers. It was immediately useful to have an extra pair of hands and eyes. However organised I am, however vigilant, I can't see or hear everything, be it coins in little mouths or a child yelling they have *"fiiiiiiinished"* on the loo.

Eszter became an integral part of our family and slotted into the fabric of our crazy world with energy, optimism, and amazing flexibility. Her working hours changed from one week to the next, and yet she remained unflustered and upbeat. She was honest and willing, unfazed by our family, and she danced as she cleaned! Her job was to help with the run of the home, be it tidying up, bathing children, or doing the laundry. If I was around, I did the disciplining and the sorting out of problems. We worked well as a team and were both very similar in character. Having someone around allowed me to dash to the post office or run to the school first-aid room because one of the children had been stung by a bee, and it was much easier than bundling babies and preschoolers into the car.

Around this time, the band flew off to Singapore, the first of three Singapore trips that year. As soon as the guys returned, they took off again to India. While playing there they visited one of the red-light districts in Mumbai and an outreach centre called Prem Kiran, a group that rescues prostitutes and their families. Martin was certainly not aware at that moment how much this trip would affect him. Singing to crowds of thousands was easy, but walking through the slums, stepping through the sewers, and facing the treacherous conditions that some called home was another matter. Here Martin's heart truly broke. My husband was a devoted daddy to our children, but that day another little girl captured his heart.

As during that phone call before Ruby was born, I heard something urgent in his voice as he spoke to me from his mobile phone in the middle of Mumbai. As I bathed our children, working a conveyor belt of slippery bodies in and out of the tub, I heard his broken heart over the line. I wasn't quite prepared for what I heard him say next:

"Anna, we've got five children already, but I've met this little Indian girl who's eleven years old," he said. "It's stupid to even consider it, but I feel that she belongs in our family. If we don't rescue her, then she's going to go into prostitution herself. So why don't we bring her back to live with us and be part of our family?"

Normally, I would have blurted out an instant response, giving no time to filter my words before I spoke. Here I was, on my own with the kids, and Martin's calling me from another continent with a social conscience. I love this about him—*his passion and motivation*—but this was big. *This was huge.* This wasn't something to discuss over the phone. Ruby disappeared under a mountain of bubbles as we talked, and the phone kept dropping off my raised shoulder.

All I could say was, "Let's talk about this when you get home."

It wasn't until he got home and I read his journal that I began to understand the deep emotion of all that he'd experienced:

> We went to see the Prem Kiran project. I never had
> any idea how much was going to happen to me by

the time I got back on the bus. Seventy children in a single room. Happy faces, all singing. One girl can't stop looking at me and I can't stop looking at her. This girl, Farin, she's beautiful, and I know that something is happening inside me. What it is, I don't know, but I know that it's big. There's something about the life that's within her; the sense that her beauty and grace shine out above and beyond this place with its crumbling streets and open sewers.

I can't understand why my heart is beating like this, why this random eleven-year-old in a city of 24 million has just pulled my guts out. Why do I feel as though every fiber of my soul is being exposed?

Our guide, Pastor Umale, tells us that Farin's mother is a prostitute. A working prostitute. My mind and my heart beat faster. He asks us if we'd like to see what kind of places these families live in. I'm nervous, but I say yes.

I couldn't tell you about the other guys, but I guess they're feeling the same. We tread the path to the houses. They're not houses, though, they're a few bricks, a collection of pens with roofs and doors and not much else. They have taps that offer clean water at a trickle, but these homes are like nothing I've ever seen before. I'm close to being sick as we walk around, treading over sewers and feeling so dumb for wearing flip-flops. It's the spirit of the place, as well as the smell, that's getting to me, the fact that under these beds, children hide while their mothers collect a few rupees from the men they have sex with. How many times has Farin lay under the bed while her mother has worked? How many cries has she had to stifle? How many nightmares has she woken up to in her own home? Or has she left the home and wandered the streets? How much more has she seen than my ten-year-old Elle? They could be sisters, but Elle talks about becoming a dancer. What choices does Farin have? How long will it be before she becomes a prostitute?

We get back from our walk and spend some more time with the children before we leave. Farin is still looking at me. We have to go. I get in the bus to return to the hotel, and inside I'm dying. I've never felt this before. I want to take her home, to protect her. I don't know what or why or how this is happening, but I know what I feel. I feel that I'm her father.

I couldn't get Farin off my mind for the rest of the day. Today it's been no different. I wake up, and I see her. I can't get her off my mind. I'm wondering, is it possible to bring her to England, to adopt her? Is it just madness to take someone out of their own culture? I haven't even been able to talk to Anna about this yet, so how can I really be thinking about adoption? The trip ends tonight,

we're about to fly home. These are mad moments—
of tears, laughter, soul-searching—all in an airport
that's way too crowded and way too bright. I need
to get back home.

—Martin, January 2007

The children were in bed, Martin was emptying the dishwasher,
and I was making packed lunches for the next day. We didn't talk
too much that night, but occasionally he gave me a hug and then
returned to refilling and sorting the cutlery drawer. He was quieter
than usual and clearly in a different head space. I'd gotten used to
this after big trips. So all this was familiar to me.

We hadn't spoken about the conversation on the phone the day
before. And Martin seemed twitchy, like a guy about to propose to
his girlfriend. He acted overly polite and slightly awkward, like we'd
just met.

That night, the conversation was one-sided. I didn't know what
to say. I just kept buttering the bread. I felt numb. What he said was
not bad, though if I rationalised it, then, yes, I was overstretched
already. However, maybe God had a plan for us. Maybe this little girl
needed to be rescued and join our family.

My inner monologue remained unspoken. I didn't want my
words to run away with themselves. I listened more than talked; I
resisted the urge to fill the gaps of silence.

21

THE
ADOPTION
PAPERS

A photo of Farin stood on the piano: a beautiful girl with skin like velvet and eyes that shone like diamonds. This girl stirred up Martin's heart and ignited something inside him. Farin's desperate mother wanted to give her daughter away to a "better" home, and Martin thought we should take her in. I didn't know what to think at the time, because my thoughts were a jumbled mess.

He had returned from the trip ten days prior, and already the information pack from the adoption agency sat on our table. It sat in its sealed envelope, waiting for me to break the seal, to give the green light, to come to grips with the idea, to be as passionate about this as he was. But I didn't know what to feel, and I couldn't muster up a response that wasn't authentic. As we ate Sunday lunch, Martin was tearful.

"Are you all right?" I asked.

"She should be here."

"What do you mean?"

"I'm missing one of my children. She should be with us around the table."

At this moment, I lost it inside, and thoughts blasted around my head: *You're always away, leaving your five children, and you're not around for them most weekends! Now you're home, and you can't even focus on your own kids—how are you going to cope with another one? For goodness' sake—concentrate on your own family!*

But I bit my tongue and didn't say anything.

"More carrots, anyone?" I asked.

My pressure cooker was steaming, but I continued to push the potatoes around my plate, waiting to have a discussion later. This was his journey.

We finished lunch and stacked the dishwasher, and the kids ran into the garden. I looked at Farin's photo and tried to feel what he felt, but there was nothing. At the time I knew God was doing something; I just wasn't sure what it was. Deep down I knew that if God was in this, then I'd be able to embrace it.

What was Martin thinking?

The thing with Martin is this: He doesn't work the way I do, and in fact, he doesn't work like anyone I know. He has an uncanny friendship with God, an unusual sense of what God is saying to him. He appears mad and drives *me* mad at the same time, but I've learned to trust that usually something bigger is happening, something that isn't always clear in the short term.

So we tried to be patient. We talked about the prospect of adopting Farin. I saw his passion and still felt nothing but eventually agreed that we should take the first steps with the adoption agency.

So we decided to open the envelope and educate ourselves in this uncharted territory.

Martin had been on the phone to India all week, trying to understand the legalities of bringing a child to the UK. There were mountains of red tape, and we were told that the process could take eighteen months or longer, with no guarantees that it would end well. We would have to pass rigorous tests in which the agency would inspect everything in our life. It was an extensive procedure, and we had to be prepared to pay the price in more ways than one. We set the wheels in motion and faced more phone calls, more lying awake at night, and more need for clarity.

Then, out of the blue, Martin took a difficult phone call. From his journal:

> I spoke to Pastor Umale today. It's been something like six weeks since I met Farin. Her mother's changed her mind. She doesn't want to let her go. First she did, but now she doesn't. What do I feel? I really don't know. Relieved? Yes. Lost? Yes. Hopeless? A little. Angry and determined and desperate? All of the above.
>
> So we make a decision that if we can't adopt her, then let's play our part in taking care of all seventy kids that live there. But there's more to this, somehow. I know there is.
>
> —Martin, February 2007

In March, Farin was still very much a topic of conversation in our house. Martin constantly talked about her and wrote songs about her. It felt odd because there wasn't any real closure. It was hard when he focused so much on this little girl when we're the ones in his life, right here, right now. However, there was peace in our home.

Umale's phone call closed one chapter and opened a fresh one for Martin. Things came into focus for us. These seemingly disparate elements—Farin, the songwriters' retreat, helping to ease the strains of poverty—were all part of the same story. The idea that art could make a difference, and that by raising money we could rescue people from oppression—this was to be the heartbeat of the songwriters' retreat.

It all started to make sense. Slowly, I realised that the only way Martin would've grieved for people in poverty was if God got to his heart. God got his attention. God spoke to Martin's heart and made him feel as though Farin was his own daughter. A bigger picture slowly developed, and now I was with Martin all the way.

The next couple of months were busy, busy, busy.

Martin finished some preproduction melodies and lyrics for the new Delirious? album, the spring American tour was coming up, and we all looked forward to Easter and our "birthday" month. Then, after many negotiations, phone calls, and scribbles on the calendar, they decided to embark on a summer tour to Asia. The guys had been invited to play concerts in India, Cambodia, and Singapore, and they wanted the families to join them to experience the things that had touched their lives firsthand.

We had to get more immunizations (ouch!) and buy twenty-seven plane tickets (double ouch!). We all waited in anticipation.

Little did I know that the experience would change our family forever.

22

PANTS AND PASSPORTS

Tonight is the last run in five before we return
[from the USA] to the UK to pick up the girls
and then fly back on Thursday. Two days to
get cases, strollers, car seats, sunglasses, and
bags of adventure packed. We then start twenty
gigs down the West Coast and then through
the U.S. Three tour buses, twenty-five adults,
and seventeen children; two skateboards, loads
of footballs, and a high chair for Ruby.

—Martin, American Tour Diary extract, April 2007

We are so grateful that we have this
wonderful opportunity of doing what we love
doing best with those we love best.

—Tim Jupp, keyboard player

Accompanying Delirious? on their international tours has been a
rich experience for the families. The tours were synonymous with

139

treasured memories, extended friendships, and a unity felt by everyone on the buses, and each tour added a photo album to our collection, all of them jam-packed with memories.

At the beginning, the boys made a rule that they would not be away from home longer than ten days at a time. Amazingly, they pretty much kept to it, apart from a couple tours in Australia. This wasn't always easy or cheap, but it was a value that we see as instrumental to sustaining healthy marriages and preserving family time. So how does a band tour America with a rule like that? Simple: You take along five wives, seventeen children, six crew members, and someone to organise it all.

Welcome Ian Cattle, the captain of the touring ship, the man who made this huge logistical project look like a walk in the park with his military-like attention to detail.

He's a man with no kids who is strangely attuned to the concerns of a mother, all while keeping the guys on track. Whether he dealt with the front of the house, amp leads, broken guitar strings, mealtimes, catering preferences, or baby earplugs, Ian waved his magic wand and had it all covered—so long as you stuck to the itinerary, and just as long as you weren't "late for the bus"! Over the years the tour grew, and not just with the rising number of venues, but also with the Delirious? women busy reproducing. What started as one tour bus became three, accommodating five families and six crew members for four weeks across America.

In later years, with the family expanding, Martin packed his suitcase two nights before any trip, which we found helpful in making the most of the last day together. For Martin, packing was methodical and minimalist. He made an art of squeezing his clothes, washbag, and running stuff into several small zip-up bags—his suitcase, when opened, always looked a little like a camping shop!

Packing for our family was a similarly methodical procedure. Packing for at least three weeks in a foreign country was a systematic weeklong activity. For starters, travelling thousands of miles every day, we often faced extreme weather changes. It might have been snowing in Denver, stormy in Tulsa, and hot in sunny California. This was often a bit of a challenge because we had to pack for any eventuality but were confined to limited space on the tour bus. In addition, suitcases were often inaccessible, as they were tucked away in their luggage bays below the bus. So I'd better have what I needed inside the bus, diaper or no diaper (we call them diapers when touring America!)—and I was left hoping that the commercials lived up to their claims of "guaranteed to keep your baby dry till morning."

However, over the years, we mastered the art of tour-bus living. We learned from our blunders and established a packing regimen that works like a dream—it all starts with purchasing a gem of a product: *the linen bag*. Every member of our family has a linen, zipped storage bag, each with their name and own emblem on the outside—Elle is a flower, Noah a boat, Indi a heart, and so on. This bag came in handy when the suitcases were stashed out of reach, so we still had what we needed.

In our packing regimen, I laid each linen bag open and covered every inch of our bedroom floor. As clothes were washed and ironed during the course of the week, I put them inside the bags until each child had five pairs of pants and knickers (underwear), five pairs of trousers, five pairs of socks, jeans, jumpers, and a waterproof jacket. One time we arrived in America without Noah's Manchester United football shirt. After a few tears (from Noah) and interrogation (by me) I realised it was hanging on the football goal in our garden, stolen from the linen bag during one of his football frenzies. We tried consoling an English eight-year-old with a New York Yankees jersey, but let's be honest—it's not red, and "Wayne Rooney doesn't play baseball!"

The rest of what we need goes into the main luggage:

Socks (white with a coloured mark on the label for each mini Smith) x 70 pairs

Shorts and skirts

Denim capri trousers

One really warm sweater each and vest tops and T-shirts (for each of the boys)

Jumpers and girly tops, with a dash of sparkle for the evening gigs (for the girls)

Swimwear (mustn't forget swim nappies)

Collection of shoes (wear trainers to the airport, one other pair of shoes each, and flip-flops, although most of the time though they run around in bare feet—I love that!)

Nightwear and slippers

Toiletries and cosmetics

Sunscreen (high factor) and after-sun lotion

First-aid kit

Pack of nappies and wet wipes (enough to get by until we arrive—four packs)

Each child also brought their own backpack and was responsible for the contents. Here are a few of my extras for the children's backpacks:

Notebook and pens (crayons for the little ones)

Nintendo DS for the older kids

Small toys

Books

Sweets (candy!) with no artificial colourings or strong
flavours (nonnegotiable! I once made the mistake of
bringing milk chocolate when Indi was small, and she
wore most of it on her hands and face, which distressed the
businessman sitting next to her!)

In my cabin bag I usually packed the following:

Baby outfit x 2

Vests x 2

Muslins x 2

Blanket

Moisturiser, lip gloss, concealer

Hairbrush and hairband

Nappies

Nappy bags

Wipes

Sugar-free sweets

Raisins, crackers

Magazines

Bouncy ball (light and small yet provides great
entertainment and exercise before a long flight)

Passports and plane tickets

The night before the flight, I zipped up the linen bags and put them straight into an empty suitcase. On arrival I took these out of the cases and put them at the end of each of the kids' bunks on the bus, so that each child can be responsible for their own clothes.

The night before we left, Martin brought the cases down the stairs and checked twenty times that we had all the passports and tickets. The children were always extremely excited, and that "night before Christmas" feeling came over the house with each of them feeling the need to bounce on their beds with high-pitched squeals. For me, I took a quick bath before going to sleep.

23

STARS AND STRIPES

I absolutely love life on the road. We have so many fun times and make some amazing memories. It's great to experience what our dads do when they leave England and go round the world. The two things I love about America are having a vanilla steamer from Starbucks and going to Old Navy, my favourite shop. My uncle Martin is the main singer of Delirious?. He tucks me in bed every night, which can be hilarious—it's different every evening; sometimes he whacks his head on my bunk, and his prayers can be very funny!

—Rosie Jupp, April 2007

On tour, when the alarm clock beeped in the morning it was go, go, go. The family minibus picked us up, and off we trekked along the motorway! We neared Heathrow Airport as the sun rose, and there was always a buzz of excitement and anticipation for the American tour.

Given that my husband spends a significant amount of the year at Heathrow, he enters the place with a familiarity and focus that gets him from A to B in the shortest time possible. Martin would beckon for Noah and Indi to walk with Daddy. I would take the little ones, and Elle insisted on pushing the stroller.

One thing that Martin and I agree on is the subject of children and airplanes—they don't go together. For some reason, I still expected to settle back and watch a movie on most flights. Instead there were thirty-seven trips to the toilet and a dozen limbs spread out all over me like a scene from a war movie. I often found a child asleep on my lap, removing any chances of visiting the toilet myself. So I just crossed my legs and chuckled as Martin took another child for toilet visit number thirty-eight.

Jet lag was a big part of any tour, so I made sure I did all I could to combat it. As soon as we were on the plane I changed the clocks and acted like we were on our destination time. Of course we all had moments of feeling dizzy, irritable, and fatigued, so I had to be even more tolerant than usual—and space and extra cuddles were definitely needed.

Once we got to our destination and settled into tour life, life on the road was great. We met so many friends in various places, and every year we visited those people we love. We always exchanged news and introduced the kids.

Once we deplaned, we headed straight for the tour buses. We loved seeing the buses ready and waiting, lined up, shining in all their glory. The familiar "on the road" routine kicked in, and the tour began. Most of the driving was completed through the night while we slept in our "coffin-sized" bunk beds and the bus covered miles of landscape. We drove from San Diego to Kansas City, from Salt Lake City to Nashville—we love America, and it now feels like home. My favourite state is California because I'm a "sun girl" through and through.

Our aim each day was to arrive at the venue by the time we all woke up. We were always grateful to our driver when we pulled back the curtains on the Jupp-Smith bus to find the bus sitting still. However, not every day was this simple. We've rolled into cities late due to many unforeseen circumstances: a flat tire, fuel stoppages, icy roads, or a tired bus driver. Entertaining small people was tricky in such a confined space when they had already been up six hours and were wondering when they could go to the park. So out came all the snacks, scrapbooks, and Disney cartoons to help us pass the time until the bus finally arrived at its destination. *Then the fun began!* We all took turns washing our faces, getting dressed, and using the bathroom. The kids chose hairstyles, and the girls took turns plaiting, straightening, or bunching their cousins' hair—and the older they got, the longer it took!

The guys on the crew bus sometimes skipped breakfast and slept a bit longer, but it was the highlight of the morning for little people with big appetites. The hospitality we received at each church or venue was wonderful. The setup varied every morning—from bone china and silver cutlery in one town, to paper plates and plastic forks somewhere else. We saw everything from a hot table displaying eggs cooked in every conceivable way, to a humble buffet with a modest selection of cereals and condiments. However, while the food changed from venue to venue, the servant heart with which it was offered was constant. We were always sincerely appreciative of the effort taken everywhere and the early start needed to feed the hungry hippos. On one occasion a guy stood in the rain escorting each and every one of us off the bus and into the venue for breakfast, holding his umbrella over our heads so that we all remained dry. Thank you, "Jim the umbrella man"!

It was always important for us to remain positive and cheerful; however, many times we were disturbed during the night. Not only were we representing our families, but as a group we reflected the Delirious? name and the core values for which we all stood. Of course that didn't always go according to plan. I remember the time during one "peaceful" breakfast in a church when one of my "sweet" daughters shouted at the top of her voice that "the eggs smell like daddy's feet." Martin got very angry, in a Martin-type way; our little child had perhaps touched on something that was nearer the truth than he dared admit—as some gigs got very sweaty! Still, even if it was the twenty-third breakfast stop on the tour, it was probably the first encounter with a particular church or concert promoter. So each day was important to the many amazing volunteers who grilled the bacon and made the coffee and to the thousands of fans that purchased a ticket.

I enjoyed attending the gigs and being part of the vision when I could. Every night the children joined their daddies on the stage in front of huge crowds. I remember one night when the energy and presence of God was so evident in the room, when all of a sudden Jon's son, Jackson, who was one and a half at the time, innocently stole the show with his dancing and his cool "body shapes." The children all got their three minutes of fame, and then just as quickly, they were bored and uninterested in the music. So they went straight to bed, passing the backstage security guards, who walked us to our buses with a wink and a "good night, y'all."

Safe inside our "bus world" we kicked off our shoes and relaxed, leaving the boys to do the "meet and greet" after the show.

> Each day moves on, as per usual. On bus, off the bus. Junk in and out of suitcases. Another hotel swimming pool that's too cold. Okay, we'll let children swim in hot tub instead, where they eventually break out in a terrible rash due to the heat of the water. I am the worst mother in the entire world, I think, and I swear to myself never to let them swim in a hot tub again. Until the next day when the hotel pool is too cold again and my kids are complaining so much that I let them jump into the hot tub again, just for a bit of peace. Not enough time to shower and get three kids ready, and they all need the toilet right before we are about to leave hotel. Wonderful, now we're late for van pickup outside the front lobby. Everyone is waiting, again.
>
> The band sound checks again. It's still pouring rain, and I run around with the kids, getting soaking wet. All of us in bare feet—I love that, I love bare feet. A highlight for me is dinner and the "Word of the Day," where we all got together to reflect on the day and pray.

—Kristen Thatcher, March 2007

So, the tours come and go, but the one trip I won't forget was in 2007, when I found out I was pregnant with my sixth child.

24

EGGS BOILED DRY

This pregnancy was perhaps the most well planned of them all. During our calendar preparations for the year Martin and I discussed the idea of a sixth child and decided we were both up for one more. Sitting at the dining table with the calendar in front of us, we worked out when might be a good time to start trying.

Very romantic, I know!

The children thought the star on the calendar was pocket-money day—if only they knew! With the summer trip to India locked into the schedule, I felt nervous about getting pregnant around that time. Memories of the flight when I had miscarried felt too raw. Also, the thought of feeling nauseous in the intense heat of Mumbai didn't sit well. The best window of opportunity was around the time of the American tour, but baby making would be tricky on a tour bus!

A week before we returned home from the States I thought maybe I had a bun in the oven. During a shopping trip to a Walmart in the middle of Texas, I managed to whiz to the checkout, hide a pregnancy test kit under some popcorn, and pop it in my bag with the speed and swiftness of a professional thief (although I did pay for it!). Then I went off in search of the nearest restroom. I was elated when the stick turned blue! I left the bathroom and bumped straight into Stu G's daughter Eden, so hurriedly I wrapped up the stick with paper towels—only two people knew, me and Jesus!

I decided not to share my news with anyone until the trip was over. I didn't want people fussing over me and certainly didn't want to distract Martin from the job he was doing. So I kept a low profile and decided to tell him once the tour was over.

Back on British soil, I let the father-of-six-to-be in on the news. Martin was overjoyed and ecstatic, but when he realised that I'd known for nearly a week he was none too happy (and still isn't!) with yours truly for keeping it quiet for so long. My expectations for that moment were for something like in the movies, where I would fall into his arms and he would swing me around in a bubble of happiness, but instead it was a bit like popping champagne to find it had no fizz. He was elated with the news but then rattled because I hadn't told him sooner, and an argument started brewing. *Please not now; this isn't how it's meant to be,* I thought. It wasn't intentional, but I'd messed up this "movie" moment and hurt his feelings. But we were supposed to be eating lunch, and I needed to rescue the eggs that had boiled dry in the pan.

The academic term that followed was packed with school and church events: outings, reports, parents' evenings, and summer gatherings with enough decorations to line the whole village. Sports day at the school is one of the most ridiculous days of my year—I do more running than the children and always vow not to wear cumbersome shoes because they usually end up discarded at the bottom of the stroller as I try to sprint barefoot around the field. One moment I'm cheering on a five-year-old in an egg-and-spoon race and the next I'm leaping to the 100-meter sack race. This year was no different—and there was no time to relax, as I was off to watch the three-legged race and trying to pacify Ruby, who was constantly trying to wriggle out of her harness. We're quite a competitive family, so it's no wonder that by the end of the day my throat was sore from all the shouting.

There were just a couple of weeks left of school, and the house was still relatively quiet. So I had some time during the day to disappear upstairs and start to get my head around packing for Asia.

25

THE RUBBISH DUMP

Having top twenty singles on the charts was a good part of the journey, but going to a slum in India and singing "Rain Down" to those who own nothing is something extraordinary, a gift that Radio One could never give us in a million years.
—Martin, 2007

At 3:15 p.m. the school doors opened, and the playground erupted with children. Every child was laden with project books, artwork on sugar paper, and gifts in abundance. Teachers wore tears, smiles, and a glint of relief in their eyes as they released their pupils into their summer holidays, hanging up their whistles for a few well-deserved weeks of time off.

A whole six weeks without school—the elation in the Smith house was tangible.

We weren't following the normal routine this year—this summer would be different. We were accompanying the band on a tour of Asia. It was a logistical headache, and I was five months pregnant, but we were very excited. This was a chance for the wives and children to see the places that had captivated the hearts of the guys. Our family planned to spend a week in India, five days in Singapore, then on to Cambodia, and finishing with a bit of summer holiday time in Bali. So it was time to get the suitcases out and read through Ian Cattle's itinerary, which looked exhausting before we'd even begun.

My dad drove us to the airport, and all of us, plus our eight heavy suitcases, fast-tracked through all the checkpoints and lines. We arrived at Hyderabad at night, stepping off the plane and into a suffocating blanket of heat and humidity. Hundreds of people crowded the streets, waiting for business partners and loved ones at the airport. The airport was a scary sight after the long flight—the stench, noise, and oppressive heat were far from the images of India I had envisaged. Holding tightly to little hands, we maneuvered our way through the crowds to our car. The drive immediately revealed the appalling conditions people lived in, and the observant little eyes of my children were wide open, taking in the poverty all around them: beggars banging bottles on the car window, children asking for food with lifeless babies in their arms.

Why had I brought my children here?

As we neared the city centre of Hyderabad, the intensity and noise escalated, and we tried to digest this foreign culture. We watched through the windows in silence, saw people sleeping on roundabouts, women digging on building sites with their bare hands, families camping on the roadside—all of this just nine hours away from our home. We stayed with our friends Scott and Melody

Norling, who came to India twenty-five years prior as missionaries and now give their lives every day for the Indian people. They're an amazing family whom we admire greatly, and their hospitality overwhelmed us. We reached their house, and I attempted to get five excitable children to sleep.

The next day was one of my favourite days ever.

We piled into a van and drove outside the city to one of the biggest slums in the area. When we arrived, we got out of the vehicle and were greeted by hundreds of little brown faces, all children running up to us with huge smiles. Here we were, Martin and me and our five kids, a thousand miles from home, and yet we'd been welcomed like long-lost friends. We were led to a ramshackle building that was the equivalent of our local village hall. My mouth dropped as we entered.

Inside, hundreds more small children waited, joy and delight radiating from their beautiful faces. We squeezed into the tiny, hot room, and immediately a whole chorus of children started singing. We wept. I'll never forget that moment. The Indian children had rehearsed songs for us to hear, all of which were beautiful and so melodic, without an instrument in sight.

The monsoon rain started to drum furiously on the corrugated roof just as they asked us whether the Smiths would sing too. There was only one song for the moment, and although our rendition of "Rain Down" was a bit dodgy, the Indian children loved to watch our children dance. The children joined us as we sang, and there lifted a beautiful harmony of voices blending nations and cultures together, loving one life, praising one heavenly Father God, all sensing the wider family of God.

Rain Down

Looks like tonight, the sky is heavy
Feels like the winds are gonna change
Beneath my feet, the earth is ready
I know it's time for heaven's rain
It's gonna rain
It's gonna rain again

'Cause it's living water we desire
To flood our hearts with holy fire

Rain down, all around the world we're singing
Rain down, can you hear the earth it's singing
Rain down, my heart is dry but still I'm singing
Rain down, rain it down on me

Back to the start, my heart is heavy
Feels like it's time to dream again
I hear your voice, and yes I'm ready
To dance upon this barren land
Hope in my hands

Do not shut, do not shut, do not shut the heavens
But open up, open up, open up our hearts

Give me strength to cross the water
Keep my heart upon your alter

Give me strength to cross this water
Keep my feet don't let me falter

Martin Smith and Stuart Garrard, "Rain Down," *World Service* © 2003 Curious? Music/Kingsway Music

At lunch I watched as Elle, Levi, Indi, and Noah helped serve huge tin bowls of rice and curry to the multitudes of children. To see my own children serving others was the greatest gift, something that I'll treasure forever. I smiled as Levi pointed out the similarities they shared: "Mummy, they're leaving their vegetables!"

Starving children still picked out their peas and put them aside— children will be children! Ruby was having a siesta; Levi had rice stuck to his cheeks; Indi observed from the side, taking everything in; Noah served curry like a gentleman, with his England football shirt on; and Elle beamed from ear to ear as she participated in this wonderful picnic. All of this took place inside a tin hut sweltering with heat, as fans whirred and flies swarmed through the tiny windows with bars. We communicated with a smile or by holding hands, and the interpreter helped out, but not much needed to be said.

> Anna was blown away. She's a mum, so it's not unnatural to be in there doing her "mum" type things—caring, loving, hugging, smiling, and pouring out compassion from every pore. Some of this stuff that's coming out of her is totally natural; some of it is completely spiritual. I think she's caught it too. I think she knows that this is something that we have to give our lives to. The kids are beginning

to understand as well. Elle's right in there, getting emotional, her heart broken: "Oh, Dad," she said to me, "what can we do?" She's right, and all our conversations are going to be different from now on. Nothing will be the same. Our actions are what count most from here on in.

—Martin, 2007

A few days later we flew to Mumbai. My mind hummed to the usual thoughts about all the practical stuff we needed for the trip. But my mind was on other stuff as well. I was anxious about what I was about to see. *How would I respond to finally seeing Farin? Would I feel like I wanted to take her home? Is that what Martin wants me to feel? Are we going to have to move to Mumbai?*

We left at 7:30 a.m. with Stu G, Karen, and the older children. We decided to leave Levi and Ruby with Eszter back at the Norlings' house. The children love Eszter and know her so well, but even though it was only for one day, it still felt odd and uncomfortable to me.

We landed in Mumbai. If Hyderabad was intense, then this place was on steroids! Everyone worked at a fast pace—people of every age swept the roads with homemade brooms. The noise was incredible: Radios, videos, and loudspeakers blared the whole time. Unbelievable smells wafted past, from the richly pungent to the delicately subtle. A million cars and tuk-tuks drove on the road. Young women stared at us, and people urinated on the streets.

Martin was excited that I would meet Farin and see the Prem Kiran project. Maybe this glimpse would help me understand a little of what had been going through his head over the last twelve months. We drove into the red-light district where her family lived. I felt expectant and nervous, yet pleased to finally be part of what had been so close to Martin's heart all this time.

When we arrived, the sky was pouring rain, and the air felt thick with dirt, grime, and pollution. It was muggy, and it stank. It felt like walking into a news documentary. As I walked, I saw such diversity and oppression alongside horrendous living conditions. It seemed surreal: Faces glared at us as we walked around, eyes surveyed our white faces with suspicion and curiosity, some looked at us with anger and some with despair—every face told a story. I felt vulnerable, especially having the children with me. How were their eyes coping with what they saw? This city was so far removed from the Western world and culture in which they live. And yet in the midst of the squalor of the slums, this was the most extraordinary place, with some of the most beautiful people that we'd ever met. It was vibrant and intoxicating. It made me feel alive.

I saw Farin, and instantly I recognised her. Immediately, I knew why all this had happened. She was so like our children: her look, her manner, and her cheeky smile. I knew why Mart felt all these feelings, and I suddenly understood and felt guilty for being so dismissive about the emotions he felt.

But at the same time I didn't want to take her home. I saw the way she was with her friends and saw the community around her. She was being looked after and was well and happy. There was a little boy on the corner that didn't look happy, and my heart went out to him. But we couldn't take him back with us either. My thoughts began to swirl in my head. *If anything, we need to move out here,* I thought. I pondered this for a few minutes, but at the time I had five kids with a sixth on the way.

What's God saying to us? I wondered. *I'm called to be Jesus' hands and feet—is this what it means? I just want to be obedient.*

We left the older children with Hannah and Lauryl (the beautiful Norling girls) for a couple of hours, and Martin, Stu, Karen, and I ventured through the red-light district. We walked in the pouring monsoon rain and saw glass and condoms littering the streets, kids walking up and down, waiting for business.

Arriving was difficult, but leaving was much harder. We kissed Farin and said our farewells until the next time. As we took our leave of this place, I reflected on all that I experienced. Deep down, I had always been a little jealous of Martin's travels and experiences around the world, especially his contact with people in extreme poverty. But when I went there and stood face-to-face with it, with the smell in my nostrils, part of me wished I hadn't seen it. I wished I could pretend I didn't know about that place, those people. I didn't want to go back—my heart was breaking. God broke my heart.

Our time in India came to an end, and with a mixture of emotions we flew to Singapore, where the band played a gig. The extremes were unbelievable—one minute we walked through open sewers in India, and in the next we drove past the Gucci shop on Orchard

Road in Singapore. Those two worlds collided for me, and my head tried to process it all.

From there we flew to Cambodia to be a part of a Joyce Meyer mission event—she often invited the band to play before she spoke. Delirious? have been honoured to serve Joyce and help get her message to the world. As part of her work, she pours millions of dollars into local projects, from orphanages to feeding programs, schools to hospitals. Seeing her work has been a huge inspiration to us. That week she came to Phnom Penh, and we geared up for a huge concert in the Olympic stadium.

One afternoon someone took us outside the city to the local rubbish dump for an experience we'll never forget. We arrived and found hordes of people, young and old, rummaging through the debris in bare feet, attempting to find something they could sell. We watched kids with open sores pick out food and clothes from the trash heaps. The place absolutely stank, and the thousands of flies spread untold diseases—this was hell on earth. It was pitiful. It was disgusting. It was wrong. These people lived here—this dump was their home. I felt sick.

Our children looked on in disbelief, in dismay that even the animals in the London Zoo lived better than this. How were they going to digest all this? What was going to be written in their "holiday news" updates at school? We returned to our plush hotel and felt guilty for taking a warm shower, drinking clean water, and eating cold ice cream. We continued to live between the poverty and the five-star dream, and it messed with our heads big-time.

The concerts didn't go according to plan. The government was unhappy about the mission work and ordered the police to intervene.

The police repeatedly threatened to close the event down and midway through one of the Delirious? sets the police pulled the plug on the power, plunging the stage into complete darkness.

Martin felt it was premature to leave the stage, so he got out his acoustic guitar and walked into the crowd. He then led the people in song, accompanied by Darlene Zschech on a megaphone. Even Joyce Meyer broke the rules and joined in. With no electricity and no PA system, a thousand voices sang together in complete darkness. It was a spine-tingling moment that helped make sense of our confusion. The crowds stayed put and cheered for more! We saw so much passion amidst the poverty, so much worship despite the oppression. I held my children close and wondered whether my husband would spend the night in a prison cell.

26

PARADOX

We arrived home just in time to buy stationery, supplies, and shoes for the new school term. The children had spent most of the summer barefoot or in flip-flops, and I hadn't noticed that their feet had grown considerably.

Sometimes my life is a parade of many paradoxes—one minute I'm weeping over children who walk barefoot on trash heaps, the next I'm spending far too much on brand-new school shoes that may only last two terms. In the space of a single day I can feel distraught over the plight of the children in India, and later I'm worried that a few grey hairs are poking through and wonder if I should visit the salon again. Hmm, what shade should I pick? Hmm, the mothers at Prem Kiran need medical supplies—now there are two sets of conversations living inside the same head.

Pillow talk with Martin changed from day to day. One moment we talked about selling everything we had and living in a van; the next moment we were excited about buying a beach hut on the seafront, which the kids would love. *Paradox.* I didn't have any answers,

so we had to live in the tension. Where there is tension there is movement. Where there is movement there is life. Where there is life there
is love, and love must be at the centre of every decision we make. It's
our motive for doing something that counts, and we must all walk
through the complicated maze of trying to use our lives to benefit
others, to give away what we've been given.

I've seen people in slums hungrier to own a DVD player than
feed their kids, and I've met millionaires who share *everything* they
own. There are wealthy people who squander every penny they earn on
themselves, and there are poor families who'll give someone their last
bit of food because that person is the guest of honour. Money is sel-
dom the issue; it's our heart that usually messes things up. Our hearts
need a revolution, and God can use good hearts to change the world.

We celebrated Indi's birthday with a houseful of girls, and after
all the presents had been opened Martin went back on the road to
America. I'd like to tell you how I exercised huge amounts of patience
and tolerance, but the ninth commandment tells me not to lie! I'm
pretty upbeat most of the time, but when I get rattled, I get feisty.
Martin and I tend to argue about the same thing—basically, I ask
him something, and he doesn't hear me, or I pour my heart out, and
he falls asleep. In our marriage this has been the one bugbear that can
drive me to distraction. I don't want to have to *ask* Martin to clean
the high chair; I want him to *see* that it needs doing. He'll always say:
"Babe, tell me what to do, and I'll gladly help." Which is great, but
I don't want to feel like I'm a wife who is constantly barking a list
of errands: "Can't you see those toilet-paper rolls at the bottom of
the stairs? They aren't going to bounce upstairs of their own accord,
honey."

Martin is always full of ideas, and his creative world often distracts him. He can wake up with an idea and by lunchtime it's in place, and new dreams and concepts just keep coming. Sometimes, though, as a product of our busy life, two weeks will pass, and he's talking about studios and websites and recordings and he's left me behind. Somehow he's got to learn to go from "Planet Martin" (the name Martin actually means is "man from Mars") to "planet kitchen." Sometimes he needs to turn his phone off and look at me with those bottomless eyes and tell me what he's dreaming about. Communication is the key. I love my mystery man, but sometimes our lifestyle can pull us apart. At times it feels like two single people living under the same roof—devoted parents with a terrible sense of disconnection with each other. We love each other immensely, but just like everyone else, we have to fight for our marriage. We're not invincible. We have to fight for what is good and right.

So this wasn't the time to withdraw or to have a critical, fault-finding spirit. I had to dig deep in the well of God's agape love, to try and model His understanding to the children and to my husband. The vision for the songwriting retreat meant that the phone rang twice as much and our life seemed to have no on/off button. We love to go, go, go, but it began to feel like things were spiraling out of control. The children began to ask where Daddy was, and as they got older they simply needed him to be around. Indi became more emotional, and Noah needed more consistent time with his father, talking and playing football. Something had to give. But we remained calm—I've learned over the years that flapping around and stressing out gets us nowhere.

Paradox.

What brought blessing and inspiration to thousands of people around the world also brought pain and resentment to our home. The band was always an extraordinary force for good, but our marriage, our children, and our family were important too. I'm all for paying the price for being "world changers," but our first priority had to be our family. In the midst of all this I saw so many positives: Our children grew up learning that we all have a "wider" family to take care of too, which gave them a more expansive perspective of their roles as human beings. I'm in awe of all of the band's achievements, and through it all they have stayed humble and down to earth, but as five wives we missed them. I missed my man. I missed his touch. I missed his smile. I simply missed him.

So with the band so busy and Martin away, everyone had to help. Elle answered the phone with Ruby on her hip while someone else cleaned up the toys in the garden. If Ruby needed help on the toilet, then Levi might take her and make sure she turned off the tap. It was a hectic time. I continually juggled five children and coped with a growing tummy, often with a houseful of cousins and friends. My grandma broke her wrist around this time, so several times I escaped from our houseful of people, people I didn't even know sometimes, and rushed out with the children to visit her at the hospital. Opening our home to various people didn't stop, but everything was more last-minute than it had been in the past. I regularly bought a sack-load of spuds to make sure all who entered our house went away fed—friends, cousins, sisters, parents, and workmen have all tasted the slightly frazzled jacket potatoes.

When Michael W. Smith visited, he politely ate his thrown-together meal, commenting on the awesome food. The truth came out when he asked for a steak knife to chisel through the rock-hard, overcooked potatoes. Another time Martin came back from touring late one night and helped me prepare for the thirty women who were coming around at 9:00 a.m. the next morning. In the depths of a pitch-black night we erected a gazebo in the garden and cried with laughter when we came down the next morning to discover we'd assembled it the wrong way up—a mixture of female brain and jet-lagged man at their best.

During this time the idea of gathering all our songwriter friends gained momentum. We decided to call the project CompassionArt. Administrative help was on hand in the shape of Paul, who moved into the playroom with a new desk, computer, and printer, nestling in the corner among Ruby's dress-up clothes. She didn't seem to mind Uncle Paul being there; in fact she loved it, often playing with her dollies on the floor while important CompassionArt meetings were being held with international CEOs. She loved having Paul at her disposal, especially when she wanted the buttons fastened on her Snow White costume.

There were other things changing at this time too. Friend and brother-in-law Stew Smith felt it was time to pass on his drumsticks and face new challenges. He had been part of Delirious? ever since the first concert in 1992, and his departure would be a huge loss. Was this the time for everyone to pursue something new, to draw a natural end to the band? How could something so amazing just end?

27

RED TAPE

Compassion: n. sympathy for the suffering of
others, often including a desire to help

Art: n. the creation of beautiful or
thought-provoking works

It was 2007, and Martin and I were both busy with the CompassionArt
project. We wanted to encourage a movement that joined the dots
between art and poverty. We wanted to help breathe life into some
of the poorest communities we'd visited, restoring hope and igniting
justice. It was increasingly difficult to see this desperation and just to
return home and get on with life. Our hearts had changed, and we
needed to act.

It all started with late-night discussions and a sense that music and
justice should work hand in hand—and now things moved forward
in earnest. We'd seen the impoverished conditions that choked and

suffocated life, yet we'd also seen remarkable people doing remarkable things to break the hold of poverty. Martin was on fire, and he had a plan. And I was so excited to be part of the vision and to be dreaming with him. I loved that on this project we worked together as partners.

Once all the musicians committed to being part of the songwriters' retreat, we faced the uphill task of speaking to their publishers. Our first and perhaps most significant phone call was with Bill Hearn, CEO of EMI Music in Nashville. Martin asked Bill to allow all the artists to be released from their publishing contracts so that the copyrights of the songs could be owned by this new charity. This would mean that all the royalties could be given to those living in poverty. This was radical—*a big ask*—and we had lengthy discussions and various meetings about everyone bucking the system. Bit by bit the seven major publishers agreed, and all twelve artists were released to be a part of this venture. At times we felt like David the shepherd boy holding a stone and a sling, standing against this modern-day Goliath. But instead of having us slay him, he bent down, picked us up, and carried us, opening all the doors we needed to walk through. *Amazing!*

Now I'm not one to be talking about contracts and copyrights, but let me explain how monumental this all was. Whenever a song appears on a CD or is played or sung publicly, on the radio or in church, that song generates royalties. A royalty is a small payment: It can be a small percentage of the price of a CD or a fee paid by a producer for using it in an advertisement or on a TV show. If a song is sung in church, that church pays a small fee to an organisation called the Christian Copyright Licensing International, otherwise known as CCLI. (Bored yet? Hang in there!) These CCLI monies are then added up and distributed to the songwriters. Before the songwriters see a penny, however, the songwriter's publisher takes a cut, and managers, agents, and sometimes lawyers take a cut. There's nothing necessarily wrong with this system, but we knew we needed a new way of raising the most money possible from these songs.

So we had a great team of artists ready to give away their own songs, their own art, to help change people's lives. It was a miracle, and it was awesome—we had found a small way to help people living in oppression and poverty. Martin and I wanted people to see CompassionArt for what it was, for these songwriters to catch the vision with us. Life is about giving, and this was the backbone of the whole project.

The date for the retreat was set for January 2008. Arrangements were made with our good friend Jim McNeish for us to stay at his old hotel on the shores of Loch Tay in Scotland. He had opened a retreat centre called the House of Cantle, where he ran training courses for businesspeople. It was the perfect place: great accommodation, space to write, beautiful landscape, and miles from anywhere.

Things got very busy, and we were spinning so many plates that there was a hubbub of activity coming from every direction. Life felt purposeful and swift, and we knew we were on to something. We were determined not to let the complicated logistics of setting up a global charity scare us. God was bigger than all the red tape and excessive paperwork.

In the months ahead our ideas gathered momentum. We made trips to Nashville, and meeting after meeting took place with managers and record labels. The journey had started. Nobody would gain financially from this project, and we had the right names on board to push it through. This project grew, our life expanded, and in the midst of it all, my little bump got bigger too.

28

OUR CHRISTMAS GIFT

The three great essentials of happiness are: something to do, someone to love, and something to hope for.

—Anonymous

There's nothing like feeling ahead of the game when it comes to the countdown to Christmas, and this year was no exception. On top of the general craziness of the season, we stayed busy planning the rooms, menus, and schedules for the CompassionArt songwriters' retreat. Gone are the days when I rushed to gather last-minute essentials on Christmas Eve. Now I'm one of those people who gathers gift ideas and makes early purchases while the sun is still hot and the back-to-school merchandise is fresh in the stores.

However, before I get too smug I'll tell you about one occasion when my early preparations truly bit me on the bottom.

For Christmas 2006 I was completely ready for the celebrations, fiercely determined to enjoy the magic of the season without stressing out too much. I finished my Christmas shopping and got the presents all wrapped up and stashed in the attic way back in August or September. Leading up to the big day I was calm, and we attended nativity events with an air of quiet confidence that everything was taken care of in the Smith home.

Christmas Eve arrived, and the mince pies were ready at the foot of the chimney for that all-important white-bearded man. We tucked the children into bed with their stockings laid out, each eagerly anticipating the night's deliveries. I was snuggled up on the sofa with my man, watching a cheesy Christmas movie with too much chocolate, but eventually it was time to switch off the TV and transport the Christmas packages from the attic downstairs. Martin crept up the ladder while I guided him to the whereabouts of the hidden treasures. All went quiet ... then the silence was broken with a hesitant, muffled voice from the attic: "Er, babe ... we've had visitors."

He handed the packages to me without saying a word, and I received bag upon bag of shredded wrapping paper and gifts covered in rodent poo and the stench of potent mouse wee.

We sat on our bedroom floor near midnight not knowing whether to laugh or cry. Finally, out came the tape and scraps of gift paper, and the rewrapping began. There were plastic bags full of discarded sweets and nibbled chocolate lollypops. Merry Christmas, mice. We hope you enjoyed your feast.

So maybe you're thinking that December is a good time to shop after all—but don't be silly! We fumigated our attic, and I invested in some Tupperware—but the story doesn't end there. Just after New Year's our attic was infested with large flies, armies of them, birthed from the maggots feasting on the dead mice in the rafters. Flies in my hair, flies in my pantry, wretched flies swarming when I changed

Ruby's nappy. *Hideous!* "Where was Martin?" I hear you ask. He was away, of course!

So for the Christmas of 2007, everything smelled sweeter and was as busy as ever. The band completed their European tour and recorded an album at our house. The attic was organised, and the Tupperware boxes lived out their "stay fresh" promise. The kitchen wall planner was filled to capacity with events and appointments squashed into every small date box. Heavily pregnant and with my energy levels waning, I prayed that this "turkey" would arrive on a day that wasn't filled with dance rehearsals, nativity events, and 101 other engagements. It was a minefield season, and no sooner were our coats on than they were off again—small people bundled in and out of cars, every possible unit of time filled up.

I felt a little fearful of giving birth, hoping that everything would be okay. Baby number six was due on the eleventh of December, but on the fifth of the month the birthing rumbles began. Elle and Indi were in a dance show that evening, and I was not one to miss the performance into which they had poured so many hours of rehearsal; I was on a mission to get there. Labour or no labour, I tentatively got in and out of the car, smiling as friends stroked my stomach: "Not long now!"

I knew that I was in early labour but thought I would perch at the back of the performance, thus not disturbing the show, and keep my legs crossed in the vain hope of not unsettling the amniotic fluid too much. Then, with my mission accomplished, another check on the calendar, we promptly exited with excited children. On the way home, Martin picked up a mild Indian curry from our favourite local curry house—there's nothing like mopping up some korma sauce with a delicious naan bread, and we thought that, with any luck, it might even help speed the labour along.

I may have overlooked the children's teeth cleaning that night, and I was a tad too preoccupied to properly scrub the theatre makeup off Elle and Indi's faces. With that nagging, crampy feeling invading my body, I left Martin watching the game and opted for an early night. Just before heading upstairs I popped into the downstairs bathroom, but after empting my bladder the warm sensation just, well, *kept flowing*. I wasn't sure if I was wetting myself or if my water had broken. I called Martin, who was engrossed in the Liverpool-Manchester United game.

"Honey, I think I am in labour."

I hesitated on the stairs, thinking that he might leap off the sofa like he does in one of his spectacular "leaping off the stage" moments, but no. As I began walking up the stairs, I realised he wasn't following me, so I carried on up the stairs, miffed that he preferred football to his wife!

Every step was painful, and I think my grandma Dorothy could have sprinted up the stairs faster than I did. As I entered the bedroom, water gushed out just as I stepped onto the clean cream carpet. I tiptoed across the room, grabbing a towel to soak up the water, and ran back down to Martin with towels between my legs, grabbing a few clothes on the way out.

"Mart, *I AM in labour*."

"Yep, honey, they're just about to score."

I won't tell you my colourful thoughts about where to put the remote control, but the TV went off promptly.

"Right, what do you want me to do, honey?"

Before we got in the car, I grabbed the phone and let my mum know that we were heading to the hospital and also phoned Eszter, asking her to get her nightie and sleep in the main house that night. Strangely, I felt calm and prepared. I was off to do a job, and that's where my focus lay. Martin was on the phone, cancelling an interview with a journalist for the next day, and thankfully he kept it brief. Walking carefully to the car, we left for the hospital with my labour bag packed with a few essentials:

- My birthing T-shirt (I wore the same one for all six children, and a few of my friends have worn it too). It's got a great slogan: "I've changed my mind!"
- New pyjamas for later
- CD of Gerard Le Feuvre's classical recitals
- Disposable pants (no one has borrowed these) that look scarily like a hairnet from the women at the local baker's, but essential for labour
- A pack of sanitary towels the size of a paperback book
- Moisturiser (got to have something to indulge your skin)
- A few chocolate treats to accompany hospital meals

During my later pregnancies people assumed that I'd know exactly what to do because I'd already had several children, but comments like, "Oh, it will just pop out" really irritated me. Each birth had been so utterly different, and with this one I still felt petrified.

I've never been ready for the pain of labour, and I've always shed my tough can-do optimism and retreated into a shell, asking for any help available. When I was between three and five centimeters dilated, I'd reached the limit of my pain threshold and requested an epidural.

When the anesthetist came into the room, I fell in love with him—this lovely Asian man took away the pain with one injection, using a rather large needle. This is the bit that Martin doesn't like to see. It's probably a godsend that the mothers-to-be can't see either, but it deals with the pain in such a way that we can sing "Hallelujah!" The drip was set up in my arm, and twenty minutes later all was calm and under control. Martin got a little shut-eye while perched on a plastic chair—and though he looked horribly uncomfortable, a man never dares to grumble at times like these!

We'd arrived at the hospital at 11:30 p.m. At 1:40 a.m. on the sixth of December 2007, Sally, our lovely English-rose midwife, delivered our new baby girl into our arms, all amidst the ambience of Gerard and his orchestra.

Welcome, Mary-Anna Merciful.

We were left alone for a couple of hours, looking upon our eight pound, three ounce miracle, thanking God for her little life. In the early hours of the morning, while the world slept, Martin kissed his girls and disappeared down the corridor to return home.

> 4:00 a.m., just got home. Left Anna there sleeping with new babe. Tired, happy, awestruck, glad to be alive, proud of my wife, can't sleep so I watch the football I recorded. Kids up in two hours, they'll be blown away. You never get used to

miracles, especially a baby one. New life is sacred.

Our Christmas present just came early.

—Martin, Delirious? website

There it was in black and white for me to read—the football that he'd "recorded." And I thought he'd sneaked back in the house to get his mobile phone. You've been rumbled, Mr. Smith!

I couldn't get out of the hospital quick enough, and this time I didn't even stay long enough for family to visit. I phoned the children that morning, all of whom were eager to tell their teachers at school. Noah asked me, "Are you sure it's not a boy, mummy?"

Four girls versus two boys now; the boys were outnumbered for sure. Arriving home to banners and balloons was a welcome sight. I got home just in time to watch Ruby in her school nativity play.

Not one to let the grass grow under my feet, I resisted the urge to have a quiet evening to myself and invited friends and family over to see little baby Mary. If people were happy to make their own cup of tea and put a few nibbles out on plates, then I was happy to snuggle under a blanket on the sofa and open my home for pre-Christmas celebrations. Mary was the best gift we could have been given, a present sent from heaven.

29

HEART AND HAGGIS

Hope is hearing the melody of the
future; faith is dancing to it.

—Ruben Alves

January 2008 was hectic. Along with a new baby, we stayed busy
tending to the last-minute preparations for the CompassionArt
songwriters' retreat, which was scheduled for later in the month.

Many doors opened, and several key players helped move everything along. Bill Hearn of EMI Christian music group helped make
much of it possible. Delirious? had distributed their music to the
American market through EMI for years, so there was already a great
relationship in place. Bill put his weight behind the whole project
and made sure the seven publishers and numerous record labels were
on board. It was humbling to see the trust they placed in Martin, and
I discovered afresh the impact that the band had made—the industry
knew him, trusted him, and partnered with him in his dream. I saw
him not just as a singer, but as a leader and a man who could lead

with integrity and grace. Many times he'd worked with these artists, sent them encouraging emails, spent time listening, or championed them to be all that they could be. In this moment as the project came into focus, his friends stood by him, and it was beautiful to watch. I was very proud of him. Nothing like this had ever happened before. History was being made.

January 11 arrived, and a dozen great songwriters gathered around the dinner table at the hotel on Loch Tay. The only disappointment was that Chris Tomlin had been admitted to the hospital in America with kidney stone trouble. It was a great loss that Chris couldn't be there, but he sent some song ideas with Matt Redman, so he was there in spirit.

I wasn't there on that first evening because I didn't want to leave the children for a whole week, but I flew up with Mary, my sister-in-law Pip, and Richard Hubbard, one of the CompassionArt trustees, for the last two days of the retreat. This was the first airplane trip for Mary, who was just over five weeks old, and amazingly she slept the whole way. My mum and dad looked after the rest of the children (they stay at our house, which is so much easier).

Paul met us at Edinburgh airport and drove us out of the city to our destination near the town of Killin. As the landscape of industry faded, the rugged countryside increased, and Pip and I felt like excited schoolgirls, full of anticipation. We drove up the pebble driveway to the hotel, welcomed by the remnants of a carefully constructed snowman. The whole place looked like something out of a Harry Potter movie, and the snow on the ground made it seem even more idyllic. Jim had turned this run-down hotel into a peaceful retreat centre, right in the middle of the highlands overlooking the most beautiful loch. We were blown away by the beauty of it all, and it was a privilege to be there with these hugely talented musicians: Michael W. Smith, Steven Curtis Chapman, Darlene Zschech, Matt Redman, Tim Hughes, Paul Baloche, Israel Houghton, Graham Kendrick, Andy Park, Stu Garrard, and my favourite, Martin Smith. There was an incredible amount of talent under one roof—so it probably wasn't the best time to get my tambourine out! The accolades among the people here were 42 million albums sold, 82 number-one songs, 10 Grammy Awards, 110 Dove Awards, 2 Stellar Awards, 2 American Music Awards, and 98 current CCLI top 500 songs. But these awards meant nothing that week. They all had to learn how to write songs with eleven other people.

Every day, the musicians scattered around the house in different rooms, and all kept busy writing in groups. Pip, Richard, Mary, and I arrived just in time for a feedback session—after working together, each group would do a bit of show-and-tell. We crammed into the piano room, some sitting on cushions, others perched on the corner of the sofa, and the atmosphere was electrifying.

As I sat in this idyllic setting on the loch, with the fire crackling and lamps and candles flickering, I listened to the musicians playing their songs to the group. I sat curled up on the sofa with a tartan rug draped over me, cuddling with Mary and realising that this was a taste of heaven—I have never experienced anything like it, and the lump in my throat was surely visible. The tears flowed—it didn't take much—as the baby hormones turned the waterworks on like a tap. I looked at each of their faces, knowing that God was doing something amazing. There were no egos in the room, no one person dominating the conversation, just a group of minstrels wanting to do their very best.

Martin is great in a stadium with thousands of people, but in a small group he gets tongue-tied, so Jim McNeish facilitated the process. Jim kept a record of all the new songs and helped us remain focused on the job at hand. Everyone felt like one big family, creating an amazing time of openness that was raw and risky, which made it even better. We felt like a part of something in the making, something radical—it was compassion *meeting* art, just as we'd hoped. The songs were great. They came and kept coming, and nobody remembered who wrote which chorus or melody or hook.

Breakfast was a banquet, and Paul organised everything brilliantly. The glass frontage of the hotel overlooked the loch, and the serenity and tranquility of the place was heightened by the distant stag we saw standing on the frosted hills during our morning prayers.

We'd asked Graham Cray, the bishop of Maidstone, to lead morning devotions, and he was brilliant. Joyce Meyer was flying to India that week and so dropped in, via Edinburgh, to treat us to a thirty-minute Bible study as well. I'd only seen Joyce speak in an arena, but here she was being herself before a small crowd of twenty-five—and she was inspirational, as always.

On the last evening, when it was time for everyone to let off some steam, everyone got on their kilts and got ready to dance. (I was in my element!) Jim had organised the villagers together and rented the village hall for a *ceilidh,* a traditional Scottish gathering involving food and dance. I'll never forget the sight of all these well-known musicians dressed in tartan skirts and sporrans, jigging to the sounds of Scottish drums and bagpipes. I kicked my legs higher than perhaps I ought to have after recently giving birth, and we giggled and danced the night away. Israel looked like something out of the movie *Braveheart*, and Paul Baloche got the award for throwing himself into the dance 100 percent. Michael laughed so hard when Martin grabbed his wife, Debbie, and the two of them danced around the hall like they knew what they were doing. Everyone devoured the haggis, and the local villagers warmed our hearts.

A perfect end to the perfect week.

The flight home came quickly. I couldn't wait to see the children, but it had been an amazing forty-eight hours and a time I'll never, ever forget. The retreat had been more successful than anyone dreamed, and the next step was to record these songs. Martin asked his lifelong colleague and friend, producer Les Moir, to help book the studios and produce the record, and before we knew it we were headlong into stage two. The team had emerged from the retreat with twenty new songs, songs that we hoped would provide the soundtrack for people's lives over the coming years.

These were songs that began to answer the question "What's faith got to do with poverty?"

There was so much love and respect for each other in the room
that it felt like a safe place. It was a very unusual way to write;
we'd have two hours sitting with a couple of other writers, seeing
what came out. Then we'd gather in the library room and play the
song ideas to everyone else. There was an opportunity for people
to give feedback on the songs or suggest changes. I found it really
educational, if I'm honest, just seeing how other people approach
the art of editing a song. Some would offer musical arrangement,
while others were more concerned with lyrical content. But when
all mixed together it brought such a depth to the writing process.
All of this happened in such a healthy and ego-free atmosphere.
I think we all sharpened each other—both as songwriters and as
Christians.

—Matt Redman, January 2008

30

SPINNING PLATES

A few days later Martin and the band flew to India for their third visit. The sights, smells, and tastes drew the boys back, as well as the beautiful people. They played at an open-air festival with Joyce Meyer preaching and Darlene Zschech and the Hillsong band playing too. Martin couldn't leave, so we had to squeeze CompassionArt business around Delirious?'s already busy schedule. Martin phoned home every day, and we always had so much to talk about in our evening conversations.

"Hi, Anna here."

"Hi, babe, how are you?"

"All fine here, what you been up to today?"

"We opened a new church this morning, it was awesome! Pounding drums and flower garlands—unforgettable! It was amazing, Anna, wish you could have been here. Then in the evening we were playing under a warm Indian sky, seeing a sea of Indian faces. They think there were two hundred and fifty thousand people at the festival, jumping up and down, an incredible night. I managed to sing 'Our God Reigns' and 'Majesty' in Hindi; a bit ropey, but they clapped and cheered anyway! I hope it wasn't too far off! What are you up to?"

"Well, Mart, I sang in front of a captive audience too; it was a song from the *Annie* movie, and now I'm about to cut a hundred fingernails and toenails after bath time. Then lay the school uniforms out, make some packed lunches, and then collapse. I love you—keep bringing joy to those faces. *Sweet dreams.*"

The band returned to Prem Kiran to see their Indian "family," and the mothers and children joined them onstage that night to sing "All God's Children." Martin hung out with Farin, shared pictures of our kids, and spent time with her family. He still loves that girl. Somehow, she's part of our family even though she lives a thousand miles away. She's the reason for CompassionArt, and she's the one who broke our hearts.

Everything happened so quickly after this trip.

It was still only mid-January. Paul worked one day a week on the CompassionArt project while acting as the merchandise manager for the band the rest of the week. We felt a plethora of emotions over the next few weeks as everyone was fiercely busy, and to top it off the only week the artists could reunite to record was during the February school holidays.

Martin and I both looked forward to the holiday to catch up with each other and our kids. But alas, the treadmill was on full blast, and there was very little breathing space. Martin felt overstretched; every spare minute he didn't spend with the band he worked on CompassionArt. We had a newborn in the house, and the kids missed their dad. Just because God's in a project doesn't make it easy.

Finally, we got a call from Les Moir telling us that Abbey Road Studios in London had been booked for three days. With that in place the writers all planned to reconvene at our house for two days prior to the recording, to tweak some of the songs and write a couple more tracks to complete the record. We juggled a Delirious? schedule, a CompassionArt schedule, and the day-to-day running of a house with six children. There wasn't enough room for it all, and every possible unit of time was full.

It felt like we needed more help.

Enter Stella Coulter—a good friend of ours who came back into our lives at just the right time. Her official role was to manage things at home and take the heat out of some of our personal day-to-day responsibilities. From calling a plumber to fix the toilet to paying bills to repairing smashed windows, she became our "wonder woman"—and she instantly brought order to our chaos. She would grab Martin for twenty minutes, having affixed Post-it Notes where he needed to sign his name on a particular document.

Soon, Martin took off to Colombia and Brazil with the band. So when my children had meltdowns all at the same time, I just took a deep breath and sang at the top of my voice the first song that popped into my head.

Songs from *The Lion King, Annie,* "Thine Be the Glory," anything. And if the crying got louder, I sang louder! It was my coping mechanism, and Mary's surprised face always made the others smile and momentarily forget their traumas. If I wanted to let off steam I had to do it in the downstairs bathroom or at the end of the garden. We were all on this roller coaster and it was scary at times, but we felt the wind in our hair, knowing we were alive and living for a bigger purpose.

Next stop, Abbey Road.

31

THE BEATLES ROOM

Walking into the studios at Abbey Road is like walking into history. Martin was in the studios for the majority of the week, so with the children at home in their pyjamas, we went to London to see a little bit of history being made. Climbing up the steps to the hallowed building, we could tell that it was a well-lived-in place. Each staircase and corridor was adorned with gold discs commemorating legendary artists such as the Beatles, Eric Clapton, Sir Cliff Richard, and Take That. (While reading an early draft of this book, Martin pointed out that Take That are not legends. Well, they are to me, and they're far better looking than that John Lennon chappy!).

This was the third day of the three allocated for recording; the band were set up in studio two, the famous "Beatles Room." Every second counted.

We stood in the sound booth, which was bigger than my kitchen, watching Michael W. Smith, Andy Park, Chris Tomlin, and Israel Houghton through the glass window. It seemed completely mad that a mere four weeks ago these songs didn't even exist, and here they were recording fifteen of them. These songs came alive right in front of us. Every now and again my eyes would catch Martin's as he stood there, and we swapped a thousand words in one small glance.

> This is hard. I'm at Abbey Road Studios, and it's the first time I've been away during the school holidays in years. It feels wrong somehow, and I miss the kids more than I can say. I feel like I'm letting them down. And I know that things have started to build up, that Anna and I are feeling like we have had to carry something. We have to up our game here, to be better together, kinder, and more supportive. It takes every effort to do it. It's tempting just to get absorbed by the project, but if I don't share it with Anna, I'm just not going to make it through in one piece. The potential is amazing. For the first time in our lives, in a significant way, we are doing something together. The band has always been my thing, even though Anna has been involved. But it's different now. She loves it; we've become a team. And the future will be amazing—she's a great ambassador for the charity. Even though she's not here, I know that she is all over this project.
>
> —Martin, 2008

During the recording of the album, Noah certainly missed his daddy's football skills. I tried to play football with him in the garden, but he just looked at me funny. He knows I can't play, but we had to make the best of what we could. We knew what we were sacrificing for this, but there was joy in bucketloads. The children missed Martin, but the bigger picture inspired them beyond belief. Our kitchen table was full of exciting dialogue and big questions, and we knew that we wanted to help the kids at Prem Kiran and those in Cambodia. The children knew they were a part of something bigger, something they didn't fully understand—but it made them feel alive.

Our family would never be the same again.

The sessions at Abbey Road came to an end, and the ongoing task of picking who should sing what songs was huge. Matt Bronleewee, another well-known producer, agreed to give his time to help record some extra vocals in Nashville. Amy Grant, TobyMac, Leeland, CeCe Winans, and Kirk Franklin all agreed to sing on the record too. Things happened fast, though it took until September to finish this momentous record properly. The songs needed a choir, string section, and mixing. Our home studio was the base of operations for the next six months.

We started preparing for Stew Smith's last gig with Delirious?. The band arranged a final London show for him at the O2 Arena. Preparations were in hand to send him out in style, to honour a top drummer and friend, and to let the fans hear him belt out the favourites with all the facial expressions and physical workouts that were his trademark. We all gathered in London and enjoyed pre- and post-show parties with all our friends. Midway through the set my sister Sarah, along with Abi and Jemimah, joined Stew onstage as a vintage Vespa scooter drove on as a farewell gift. It was an emotional moment and an unforgettable night.

32

WHITE TEETH

No one person can change the world, but you
can change the world for one person.

—George Hoffman

We cannot hold a torch to light another's
path without brightening our own.

—Ben Sweetland

"We need an African children's choir," said Martin, rushing out of the studio in a frenzy. "That's what this record needs to finish it off! Let's phone Watoto and see if they can do it!"

Watoto is a church in Kampala, Uganda, that also cares for orphaned children, giving them housing, education, and health care. As part of the children's development, they sing. In fact, they happen to have amazing children's choirs. The choirs travel the world doing concerts, raising awareness of the plight of HIV-infected children abandoned by their culture. They have the most beautiful sound, and the production team thought their texture and depth would be a perfect fit.

So Martin phoned the UK-based Watoto choir to ask if they were available. Watoto has choirs based in the United States, UK, and Uganda, and naturally we thought the UK-based choir would come to the studio. Sadly for us, they had too many concerts booked. However, the choir in Kampala said that they would love to do it.

It was a Monday evening, and the house was full of teenage girls from the church youth group. The group met every week in our front lounge, in the garden, or on the trampoline. So in they came with their mobile phones and various shades of nail polish, and we sat eating M&Ms. Our conversation revolved around the latest eye candy in the classroom, alongside the meaning of the Beatitudes.

Martin walked in and dumped his luggage.

He had just returned from somewhere—Portugal, I think. He tiptoed around so he didn't disturb the prayer time. He sent me a wink across the room, and I blew him an air kiss and mouthed, *Talk later.*

We wrapped up the meeting, and I left the girls dunking marsh-mallows in their hot chocolate so I could hunt down the traveller. I found him in the dining room, typing up emails and checking the sports pages. He looked up.

"Hello, babe. Missed you," he said.

"Missed you, too. How was your trip?"

"Good, thanks … look, there's something I need to ask you. Is it possible that we could go to Uganda during the May half-term week? Perhaps we could all go? What do you think?"

The question rolled off his tongue as if he were asking me whether I wanted a cappuccino! I wasn't expecting that. I raised my eyebrows and gave him my full attention.

"Sure, I'll think about it," I replied.

"The only problem is, honey." He paused. "I need to know by lunchtime tomorrow."

Okay, now he had my *undivided* attention, for a moment anyway. I still had a house full of teenagers that weren't eager to leave—those girls can talk and talk!

As I tried to digest Martin's question, I straightened up the front room and rearranged the furniture. One by one I said good night to the girls.

Finally, I got into bed and lay there, staring into space, wondering. *Is it a good idea to take six children to Africa for a week? Is it safe? How many suitcases will I need?* Martin needed to know by the next day because airline ticket prices were rising by the day.

After a night of deliberating, we decided to bite the bullet—we were off to Africa with six children and our au pair. I phoned the doctors' and booked the children to see the nurse for that morning. We all had to get yellow fever, hepatitis B, tetanus, and diphtheria immunisations, along with a prescription of malaria tablets.

When the time came, we flew from Heathrow to Kampala, and out came the jar of Nutella. The only way I could get the malaria tablets down the children was to disguise them into a generous scoop of the chocolate spread. I'd already tried crushing the tablet into a zillion pieces, but that had failed. So, at the same time each day, out of my bag came the divine tub of hazelnut chocolate spread—one spoonful with a little white tablet in the middle for each of us. Ruby looked at me, her eyes popping out like I was now on her wavelength—finally Mummy was tuning into the delights and wishes of a two-year-old—and she became my best friend three times a day!

Uganda is a place of vast contrasts, from dusty roads to lush jungle—a country of rare beauty. Stepping off the plane, one is hit with the amazing feeling of huge space, clean air, and high heavens.

A bus full of sweaty people took us to our hotel, and we couldn't help but stare at the people while they stared at us. Men and women held chickens and carried bags full of laundry. On our first day we were fortunate enough to be flies on the wall for the rehearsals of the Watoto choir. Martin rigged up all the microphones and cords so all would go smoothly for the recordings. Children of all ages sang songs both in English and their native language. Beautiful and harmonious, the sound was full of purity and innocence and joy beyond words—and was accompanied by vibrant dancing. The African children giggled when Indi wiggled her hips and Ruby tried to sing along. I enjoyed every minute, wondering how my children would digest all that they saw here.

It was a whirlwind trip and the itinerary was jam-packed. On the second day we went on a two-hour drive out of Kampala into the African countryside. We were guests of the charity Compassion UK and had the opportunity to see all that they were doing for thousands of children and mothers who are in difficult and often tragic situations in that part of the world. Compassion provides a safe place to nurture and foster the needs of these fragile young children, and part of our purpose for being there was to learn more about how their projects worked and then to raise awareness for the folks back home.

A third reason for coming to Uganda was to film some footage for the CompassionArt documentary that would be sold along with the music CD. We wanted to show the journey from Scotland to Abbey Road, from record sales to feeding children around the world.

The cameras were zooming in on the poverty, and the lights were bright and invasive. It wasn't the time to get emotional—rather, I wanted to do something that would offer hope—yet I didn't know what to say. Words seemed futile. I just wanted to hide and hold the children. I was a mum whose heart was broken, and I couldn't bear to see those precious children without decent food and adequate clothing, so I looked into the camera and started to speak while Noah fed a small boy in the background.

Here we met a beautiful lady living in a mud hut the size of our garden shed, a mother of eight children with her ninth baby on the way. We sat hand in hand, worlds apart in so many ways, and yet we were united in motherhood. She bore the pain of her life's struggles, and we sat in silence.

The next day we visited the Bulrushes, a rescue home for abandoned and orphaned babies, run by the Watoto church. We saw children who had suffered second-degree burns, children who had been shot, and other children who had been abandoned, left on rubbish heaps. One baby caught my eye, and I was told through the translator that he'd been found in a toilet. Another boy had been found in a trash can and was literally being eaten alive by maggots—he had severe scars on his head—before he was brought in by the medical services who had tried to repair the damage. One little boy in the orphanage had been left to die on the roadside, and there was yet another child whose mother had died of AIDS. I was devastated to see these precious, innocent children discarded like trash. Where was the sanctity of life? The stories tore my heart apart.

Annie, the centre manager, was practical and down-to-earth. Her heart exposed her compassion and sincerity, and her conviction to impart change was her sole mission. These children weren't victims of their past; rather, the volunteers nurtured these children to be champions of the future.

The following day we went back to the Bulrushes—no cameras this time; we were just there to help where needed. We just wanted to lend a hand, and it was a simple task: These babies needed cuddles, unconditional acceptance, and love. It's so uncomplicated that even children can do it. We spent the afternoon giving as much as we could. There were ninety-two babies who, when ready, would be moved on to one of the Watoto villages where a "mother" would take them on as they grew. These women are often widows or victims of domestic abuse, so it's a win-win situation: The children need care, and these women need a safe place to live. It was great to see how the two centres worked together. The children stay in the Bulrushes until they're five years old, and then they're moved out to the Watoto villages.

The CompassionArt dream was to build creative centres in each of these villages so the children could learn music, dance, video editing, and more. We were shown a piece of land upon which this centre might one day be built. We all stood there and prayed that this dream would come to pass.

Later, the boys grabbed a few minutes for the all-important football match on a rickety field with three remnants of bamboo nailed together for the goal. The oppressive heat beat down upon my boys, with their England football shirts wrapped around their heads and their shoulders burning in the afternoon sun. But a goal is a goal, and joy is joy in any language.

The following day we met a woman who came from Gulu in northern Uganda just to tell us about her organisation. Her organisation dealt with the horrors of war and child soldiers. She told us about the rebels who come into their villages, abducting boys as young as four or five years old and taking them into the bush to train them to be killers. Sadly, they have started to take the girls as well, many of whom are abused and raped by the soldiers. She told us that by 2010 there will be fifty million children affected with the HIV/AIDS virus. And there was more.

We visited other communities living in extreme poverty. We bundled into the two minibuses with our tour guides and sweaty film crew. We crossed miles of dusty tracks, peering out the sliding windows. We saw mothers with babies strapped to their backs or with pots of water balanced on their heads. Levi giggled, seeing women who had "forgotten to get dressed," which sent Noah into peals of laughter.

The realisation that they had just walked many miles to get fresh water sank into our heads and hearts, and we became aware of the stark reality that one pot of sudza (a meal made from corn) was used to feed a family that made ours look small. "Only six children? Come in, sister, meet my eleven," I heard more than once.

The dusty dirt tracks led us into lush African jungles. So lush, in fact, that the wheels of Mary's stroller got caught in the mud, so the locals carried her above their heads. They were smiley, happy, and beautiful people, or as Levi described them: "lots of black faces with very white teeth!" After each venture out, we'd return to the hotel to splash around the pool and have a ham-and-cheese sandwich—such bitter contrasts.

By day five the emotion of the week started to take its toll. My children were doing well, but were getting tired and irritable in the African heat (or maybe that was just me!). However, everything we'd seen and experienced made it worth the journey.

On the final day we took our custom-made inflatable CompassionArt logo back to the Watoto village to shoot the front cover of the album. It was forty feet high and twenty feet wide. We inflated it on the piece of land that was reserved for the first CompassionArt creative centre.

I don't take it lightly that we were able to take six young children to Africa and give them this experience. We want our children to grow up with love for the unloved deeply rooted in their DNA, so they know that this life is not just about them but about serving those who need help. We flew home with ten pieces of luggage, one stroller, two car seats, and a whole lot of happiness. We transported sleeping children from the car to their beds before Martin and I collapsed into ours.

33

THE PRESS
RELEASE

I see my path, but I don't know where it leads. Not
knowing where I am going is what inspires me to travel it.
—Rosalía de Castro

Two months had passed since our trip to Africa. Mary continued to delight us, and by the end of May 2008 Stew had played his last Delirious? show. Again we found the mixture of new life in Mary and the ending of an era for my brother-in-law to be bittersweet. Stew's final show was an emotional tribute to someone who had faithfully given sixteen years of his life to serve the band. With Stew's blessing, the guys chose to carry on with Paul Evans, a younger drummer who had grown up in our church. Paul was a talented yet humble man who stepped in to fill some very big shoes.

However, something new and different began to stir inside of Martin and me. Delirious? had been the centre of our world for sixteen years, but we began to talk about how our life would look without it. The guys sounded better than ever, performing large concerts around the world with a huge following. This was almost all we'd ever known since we'd been a couple. Against this backdrop, we simply wanted to be the best parents possible, to keep following God's plan, and to sustain a healthy marriage. Martin wanted to be around more for me and the kids: for sports days, weekend breakfasts, birthdays, and bedtime stories. We knew something had to change. It was like that feeling you get when you wake up one morning and you know it's time to change jobs or paint your bedroom a different colour. But this was a huge decision to make and one that would affect a lot of people. Not something to be taken lightly.

Two months passed, and these feelings grew. Martin knew it was time to leave the band. We knew deep down this was the right decision for us and immediately felt a deep peace at letting go of something so amazing. There was no celebration, though, as it was a solemn time. This wasn't an ordinary situation—it was our family, our job; it was our life.

The next day the boys were leaving for America, and we wondered what to do. Do we call everyone? How do you tell your best friends something so important? Timing is always difficult. One of the families planned to stay in America for the whole summer, so we wouldn't all be together until September. It felt right to gather everyone face-to-face for something so big, but Martin knew he wouldn't be able to be on the road with his brothers and not be honest with them. So with cases packed again, he left for America with tears in his eyes and the realisation that this would be one of the hardest weeks of their life as a band.

Two days into the tour the boys all sat down on the grass outside one of the venues, and Martin asked to be released from the band.

He sounded very low when he called me soon after. Even he was shell-shocked at what he was doing. He was laying down something that he loved, but in the same moment he felt clear that this was the right thing before God and our family.

The Delirious? guys are five amazing men, and they weren't just a great rock band—they were like brothers, and disappointment is hard to cope with in such tightly knit groups. It would be untruthful to say that everything was a smooth ride. It wasn't. There were bumps in the road; there was heartache, uncertainty, and a tragic sense of loss. Tim, Stu, Jon, and Paul decided that they didn't want to continue just the four of them, and so they put together a statement to tell everyone their intention to end as a band. The fans needed to know.

On the sixth of July, Delirious? released a statement on their website:

> We would like to address all our fans, our friends, and people around the world who have faithfully supported Delirious?.
>
> After 14 albums, thousands of shows in front of millions of people, and many extraordinary memories, we have decided that at the end of 2009 we will take a break from recording and playing as a band.
>
> Our decision was triggered by a request from Martin to be released from the band to pursue new projects, including his work with CompassionArt and the desire to be at home more with Anna and

his children. We have of course honoured this
request and made a decision together that now is
the time to end this chapter of our lives.

We will continue to play and be excited about
our current tours and bookings but will not be add-
ing many more over the coming 17 months.

We are all so deeply grateful to our incredible fans who have sung the songs and allowed
Delirious? the privilege of providing the soundtrack
to many lives over the years. From the school hall
in Littlehampton to the stadiums of the world we
have many stories to tell our children's children.
Delirious? also would not be what it is without our
amazing wives and families, and our gratitude to
them is immense. We will now move forward to the
next part of our lives where new challenges unfold
and greater stories will be written.

We want to make it absolutely clear that
although this decision has been extremely painful and difficult, we are still great friends, and our
respect for each other is unquestionable. We love
playing in this band together and know that even
though 2009 will bring an end to this current journey, there will be more adventures together in years
to come.

We always used to say that we were "taking it
wherever it goes." The music ended up going further and deeper than we could ever have dreamed,

yet we are now at a point where our creative futures will spread out and take on different journeys.

Thanks again for believing in us through all these years. We believe the best is yet to come.

—Jon, Martin, Paul, Stu G, and Tim

So right now, our future is unknown. *Uncertain but hopeful.* I want to find a new way of living, to find a new way of life with Martin, my children, and with my heavenly Father. I want to reconnect with my soul, feel my heart beating again, and feel the breath of God flow through me.

For a family that is used to being busy, it's time for us to live a slower season. I don't mean that we'll sit on a beach for a year doing nothing (although that sounds very nice!). No, life carries on. Packing school lunches, having friends over for dinner, serving our community, providing late-night taxi rides for teenagers, watching forty kids play football in the garden, making music, and writing books. Yes, life carries on because life is always best in the context of community.

We are now in the process of finding a rhythm for the first time in our family life. We are incredibly blessed and fortunate to have a season in which to create time and space for bike rides, for candlelit beach-hut nights, for new creativity—and especially for God.

I vividly remember Martin sitting in his car many years ago, all smashed up, wondering whether he would live, wondering whether we would have a future together. I never imagined in my wildest dreams that we would be here today, looking back with so many stories of God's love and grace. Martin said that he'd been given a second chance, and we took it. *Boy, did we take it!* And now we stand again together with our six children at the beginning of a new future.

MY TOP 10 SURVIVAL TIPS

1. Attitude

Dressing myself with a positive attitude is as important as remembering to floss my teeth; it's not essential, but it sure makes a big difference, and it's a daily practice. Developing a good attitude helps keep perspective and sanity. Attitudes are the beginning of values: a sense of morals so my little ones can decipher what's right and wrong. I love what the Bible says about soaking ourselves in good values: "Whatever is true, whatever is noble, whatever is right, whatever is pure, whatever is lovely, whatever is admirable—if anything is excellent or praiseworthy—think about such things" (Phil. 4:8).

The way I approach life is seen and heard by a dozen little eyes and ears—they are watching my every move, from how I speak to the sales assistant to how I respond to the person who stole my parking space.

I know that keeping a positive attitude will get me through the day, so I try to make it as tangible as putting my makeup on. For the younger children we have fun now and again when they're getting dressed: "Socks on, check! Shoes on, check! A good attitude today, double check!"

Sometimes we choose a particular word for the day, such as *helpful, kind, generous, hygienic, patient,* or *tolerant.* I try to choose something constructive that shifts the emphasis from me, me, me, to focus on others. These are bite-size, manageable goals that work more wonders with my children than phrases like "now be a good girl," which can be too vague in my little ones' heads.

2. Positivity

I've always believed that to be positive is to be powerful. I always want to believe in what I'm doing, communicate clearly, and celebrate success—be it academic or behavioural—by praising and complimenting my children and raising their self-esteem. I believe that the only way to raise positive kids is to be a positive parent, so I think about things like: *How do I start the day? How do I finish the day? How do I respond when the doorbell rings at an inconvenient moment?*

To raise positive children I try to use the essential ingredients of love, discipline, and forgiveness, wrapped in an abundance of care and commitment. I try to be aware of negative conversations and curb negative self-talk such as, "I'll never finish this job," or "It'll probably rain." When we get positive input we give positive output, and when we have a negative input we have a negative output. Children develop who they are and gain a sense of self-worth and self-identity from the values and attitudes from those around them. The only opinion a child has of himself or herself is what they have been given from those responsible for their early development.

3. Laugh

A sense of humour is required to survive parenting. I laugh *with* the children, not at them—and I do my best to empower them, enjoy them, and have fun. Laughter boosts self-esteem, especially if the source is the child—give a child a captive audience, and something ridiculous and repetitive can send children into peals of laughter, which is brilliant entertainment while you're loading the dishwasher.

The Bible says that "a happy heart makes the face cheerful" (Prov. 15:13) and that "pleasant words are a honeycomb, sweet to the soul and healing to the bones" (Prov. 16:24). Laughter is medicine for the soul, so I try to keep smiling even when things seem crazy—so what if the ketchup spills on the rug? So what if someone didn't make the toilet in time? Life's too short to get bogged down with the small stuff, so I laugh it off, get the clumsy one to help clean up the mess, and move on—I don't need to verbalise every annoyance.

I certainly don't want my tribe to be reckless in their actions, as respect of property and belongings is important, but "accidents do happen." If someone spills their juice, they get a paper towel and help clear it up; if someone wets the bed, we take the sheets off and take them to the wash. Simple. If Mary puts spaghetti in her hair, we laugh because it's really quite hilarious, and then when she continues to do it, heaping on the sauce, I stop laughing and put on my serious, sensible hat.

4. Discipline

Discipline is about teaching and instruction. I hope that when discipline is implemented, as in punishment, a lesson is learned. I try not to nitpick too much, because there's no peace in an environment in which every comment generates tension. So I focus on what's important and screen out the rest. Being fair, firm, and consistent are the basic parental mandates—my children get confused if I'm calm one day and freaking out the next. Children love boundaries—for someone so small, the world's a scary place without them—and the children also need clear expectations that are consistently employed. I constantly ask myself: *What is the culture of my home? Is this a case of "wait till your father gets home" (which wouldn't always work if Martin was away for two weeks in South Africa)?* So I tend to discipline as soon after the offense as possible to avoid forgetfulness.

I rarely use the bedroom as a place of punishment because the hall has far fewer toys in it, and when I speak to or punish the children, I like them to look into my eyes so they can see how cross I am. I've found that while rules are important, setting a good example is better. I've also found that alongside the basic rules and boundaries, part of being a parent is allowing the children to experiment and test the boundaries. My relationship with them is the safest environment in which to do this. So I set rules, explain what they mean, remind the children what they are, and stand firm.

My general rule is to *break the will but not the spirit,* so I try to make sure they understand the reason for my disciplining them by getting them to repeat what I've said. The question "Why am I cross?" often results in a blank look, so I gently remind the child: "Because you snatched the dolly out of Poppy's hand." Then I'll ask again: "So, why is Mummy cross?" And then they understand for themselves: "'Cause I snatched the dolly."

5. Communication

I want to be someone who listens more than I talk, and I'm slowly learning how to do this! When I consider that communication is 7 percent words, 38 percent tone of voice, and 55 percent non-verbal cues, I question why I even waste my words. Sometimes they can bounce around the walls and have less effect than if I've said them in a foreign language. Is it unrealistic to think that six children will sprint to the table on command with washed hands and empty bladders and sit still without touching their forks? It's about time I invested in a gong, a whistle, or a school bell, something that will get bums on chairs quickly and stop me sounding like a fishwife.

I'm all for the approach of getting down to the child's level and giving them my undivided attention, employing active listening—truly engaging with their world and not being dismissive is essential. I may think, *Here we go again; what are the tears for this time?* But to a three-year-old my response is so important. I remember having a conversation with one of my boys every day for his first year of school when he protested about going. After his first week he commented that school was okay but he was glad that it was over. Breaking the news to him that he would be going for the next sixteen years of his life was not received well. I use lots of eye contact with the children—if I'm expressive, they will be too. Showing joy, disapproval, and surprise not only validates feelings, but it's also a great facial workout!

6. Obedience

There's never a better time to teach children obedience than in the early years. A child lives in a world of feeling and discovery rather than reason, so tone of voice, atmosphere, and physical touch all play a part. I give one instruction at a time, am specific, and go straight to the point. Then I get the children to repeat what's been asked of them, because even if I think I've made it quite clear that the play farm animals need to be put back in the box, when I ask my three-year-old, "What are you going to do now?" I get a blank look and a chewed sleeve. As tempting as it is for me to scoop the play animals up into my arms (which would take about ten seconds), I resist. If I help, I give the message that it's okay to leave the mess, because Mummy will clear it up anyway. So as painful as it is to watch how slowly the buffalo is handled, played with, and then tossed into the box, I hold back. Ultimately, I've given an instruction, and my child will see the job completed and learn obedience.

I've often used the "1, 2, better be done by 3" tactic. This method has lost its power with the older ones, but for the toddlers it's an effective way to keep my cool. Obedience is coupled with independence and self-confidence, for example, when the children dress themselves, order food in a restaurant, tell the doctor how they feel, pick their own clothes for the day, choose their own cereal, or make a decision about movies they want to watch. I help my children set realistic goals, give them positive feedback, and show them appreciation. Recently, my eldest had an appointment for a haircut, so after I made the appointment and gave her the correct money, off she went to the local salon—stepping stones toward independence. However, my second eldest might be given a different task to assert independence—as a solo trip to the barbers' could have serious repercussions.

7. Routine

It seems like a contradiction, but our routine gives me amazing freedom—it organises my daily life into manageable chunks. Our routine provides a helpful structure for nonnegotiable events such as mealtimes and bedtimes.

Every parent of small children will understand the 5:00 p.m. to 7:00 p.m. crazy hours—expect the phone to ring into the answer machine during this time, because it's feeding time at the zoo! Feeding time is followed by cleanup, bath, bed, story, milk, and "night nights." When the routine goes to plan I can reward myself with a quiet evening and a bowl of chocolates on the couch—perfect! At times, Martin may have been playing to a crowd of twenty-three thousand and the pope in Athens, but sitting in front of the TV with a bowl of treats is pretty hard for a mother of six to beat.

8. Words, Words, Words

Words fill our world. Conversations, television, advertisements, and songs flood our ears and senses. We all know that words have meaning and therefore value and power. I've learned that it's good to treat words as a gift and tame the tongue. In the Bible the tongue is likened to a bit in a horse's mouth, the rudder of a ship, and a spark (James 3:3–5); it is very small but capable of devastating damage and destruction. The Bible also says that "the mouth of the righteous is a fountain of life" (Prov. 10:11). What comes out of my mouth can be life-giving, but do my words build others up or leave others feeling put down?

Most of us think great things about other people yet never tell them, but we have to realise that praise only becomes important when we speak it. My friends are my friends because they encourage me with their words—I wouldn't hang around with people who constantly put me down. However, our words start with the heart, as Jesus said: "The good man brings good things out of the good stored up in his heart, and the evil man brings evil things out of the evil stored up in his heart. For out of the overflow of his heart his mouth speaks" (Luke 6:45). Sometimes my children will say, "I didn't mean to say that," but the truth is that their words came from the overflow of their hearts. So how I talk about someone else says more about me than that person, as my words are my advertisement to the world of who I am, what I feel, and what I think.

Every time I open my mouth to speak, I let others into my mind, revealing what's inside me. So I'm reminded to guard my words, guide my words, and give my words away.

9. Forgiveness

Everyone makes mistakes. To forgive those mistakes is the act of love. It's important to apologise to my children when I mess up, as well as to encourage them to say sorry when they mess up. Sometimes this can be hard, but Martin and I are not perfect. When we say sorry to each other or to the kids, it's a good example of modelling forgiveness and a soft heart. As a general rule, if the children see Martin and me argue, we try to make up in front of them too, so they see conflict *and* resolution. I love the way the Bible encourages us to love and forgive one another when we mess up, and I try to remember to "clothe [myself] with compassion, kindness, humility, gentleness and patience" and to "forgive as the Lord forgave" (Col. 3:12–13).

10. Time

I want to have the wisdom to know that every day I spend at home is a day with my children; that there are no unimportant moments in their lives; and that no other work is more rewarding and no task more urgent. Yes, of course my time is divided, diluted, compromised, and gobbled up, but my time is now, it's all I have, and I want to be a good steward of that time.

ANNA AT THE MANOR

Laundry, cleaning, school runs, cooking, playgroups, food shopping, clubs, church, parties, doctors' appointments—all these things contribute to the familiar pattern of life with kids, and before I know it Daddy's home with more laundry to add to the already overflowing basket. (I've been known to shrink some of Martin's stage clothes, so for what it's worth, honey, I am sorry about your green cashmere jumper!)

For me there's always a bit of intrigue about how other people manage their home life. I love systems and procedures, and I've been so inspired by many of my friends who develop their own genius ways of getting through mundane jobs. Let's face it, in the Western world we've become sofa voyeurs as we watch other people's homes to see how the professionals scrub a filthy house or reorganise someone's life. So here's a quick blitz around my house.

Laundry

In my house, washing is a military operation, and the hum of the washing machine is my constant companion. I do at least three loads a day—whites, coloured, darks, and then there's the bed-wetting incidents, and extra towels for houseguests.

I have two dirty washing bins, one for colours and one for whites. It's up to the family to put their dirty clothes in the right bin (yeah, right!). There's always the threat of pink pants for the boys if they mess up the contents of the bins! I love the way the older children coach the younger ones, who like to throw more than their dirty laundry in the bins: "Mary, Mummy's hair straighteners don't go in the laundry bin," to which Noah pipes up, "They're not Mummy's, they're Daddy's!" He likes to get a laugh whenever possible. Levi can spend several minutes studying his football shirt, deliberating if it's got more white than colour on it—he's so exact about things, it brings a smile to my face. In contrast, Ruby's clothes rarely ever make it to the bin at all; they're more likely to be tossed onto the floor or abandoned in the various rooms she's skipped into. I said I liked systems—I didn't say they all worked!

I have to admit to one of my luxuries: my tumble dryer. It's a huge shortcut and saves time when compared to hanging the clothes on the clothesline. Aside from linen, towels, and other big stuff, it all goes in the tumble dryer.

Tidying Up

Tidying up is an endless, thankless task, but I've found that investing time in organising things, labeling drawers, and marking shelves makes it easier for me. Investing a bit of time to set up systems can pay dividends later when creating an efficient and orderly environment. I think my days at the play centre have made me partial to a few labels and permanent marker pens. I can't help myself. I even have my linen cupboard labeled: single sheets, double duvet covers, and pillowcases. It does end there, though, I promise, lest anyone thinks that I have my shoes labeled in such a fashion. (Now there's a thought: everyday shoes, "blisters like small cupcake" shoes, never-wear-again shoes, strappy wedding shoes, wrong-size shoes, and "what was I thinking when I bought these" shoes.)

My rule of thumb with tidying up is never put off a job that you can do now. If I'm walking past a mess, I sort it out. In fact, I probably spend half the day scrambling around on the floor. If something is picked up, it's put where it belongs or at least dumped on its way to where it belongs.

I encourage the children to make their own beds, and on Saturday morning we do a room inspection—and the owner of the tidiest room gets the extra chocolate crepe or croissant at breakfast. While some of my children will rise to the challenge with speed and enthusiasm, others will greet the task with a measure of nonchalance—saying they would rather pass on the croissant. Noah reaps the reward by sharing with Levi, who is meticulous on things being put in the right place. Ruby and Mary, quite honestly, rarely stand a chance. No extra breakfast treat is going to entice them to sort the array of tangled beads or face their books seam side out on the bookshelf—no way! I also like the children to know where the spare toilet rolls are kept, in the vain hope that when one roll is empty they may replace it (as if!). They know to put plates in the dishwasher, not to take shoes into their bedrooms (makes it easier to find them when we're trying to leave the house in a rush), and to clean up spilled drinks, and when they have friends over they get a five-minute warning so they can tidy up before they leave. In every area I try to reinforce the attitude of "do to others as you would like them to do to you."

Cleaning

Over the past few years, an amazing lady (there have been several different ones) comes into my house twice a week, and two hours later she leaves, having worked her magic—ironing clothes and wafting the scent of Pledge polish around the house. On a daily basis I get the vacuum out of the cupboard more times than I care to mention—certainly too many times to worry about having the cord neatly wound around the hooks. In, out, in, out, sucking up a whole collection of high-chair rejects.

Food Shopping

I do our food shopping at the click of a button now. For ages I resisted the urge to order the food on the Internet, but now I'm completely converted. I may not be able to squish the bread on the bakery shelves or breathe in the smell of the ocean at the fish counter, but I can live without that when someone handpicks my food off the shelf and delivers it to my door. This method is so much better than piling six children into the car, racing round the aisles, trying not to lose the stragglers while watermelons fall out of the loaded shopping cart—online shopping is money well spent in my book. With all the comings and goings in our house, I'm so used to catering for the masses that I can never just buy one of anything—I always like to make sure I have enough to pull a meal together for unexpected dinner guests.

Cooking

I usually cook a Sunday roast and a pasta bake of some description in the middle of the week. Friday is pizza night, and the week wouldn't be complete without a baked potato and various fillings. I tend to cook for the five thousand, and I'm not too hot on using rubber bands on packets, so if I open a bag of pasta it all goes in. Sometimes there are leftovers, but more often than not someone will need an extra snack from the fridge later in the evening. I try to teach the children the food groups: carbohydrates, proteins, and the other nutrients, otherwise Noah would eat a whole pack of strawberries or pile a mountain of Weetabix in his bowl. Also, I like to plate up the kids' food so I can see what's being eaten and by whom. Buffet style doesn't work well because I never know what each child has eaten. I try to remember that after Martin returns from a trip to Germany to go easy on the ham sandwiches—as much as he loves them, he's usually had his fill of continental meat and cheese unless he's on a high-protein diet.

Clothes Shopping

Not surprisingly, there isn't much time for clothes shopping. The thought of taking six children to a shopping mall is my ultimate nightmare. I avoid the stress and, instead, four times a year (every new season) when the children are at school I dash out to the

Southampton Shopping Centre for a quick blitz. A vanilla latte and scone are a must on these trips, and once satisfied we hit the shops. I go with what I know and am a bit of a creature of habit when it comes to where I shop. Elle dresses herself; she's got great taste and coordinates well. She loves skinny jeans and Ugg boots, and her style is a cool bohemian look—she loves anything that Kate Moss wears. Indi wants to look pretty but spends most of her time doing cartwheels, and so we've got to buy practical. The boys are easy and mostly, when not in a school uniform, favour their sports outfits. Hand-me-downs are great, and I love a good rummage in the charity shops when I have the time.

Simplicity is the key for me. Take underwear, for example: I buy white socks and pants and mark in coloured pen on the label to indicate which pair belongs to each child: blue for Levi, green for Noah, red for Elle, etc.

QUESTIONS

How do you spend quality time with each child?

Spending quality time with each child is something that I try my best to fulfill. Bedtime is a good time for this—each one chooses a book to share with Mummy, and we spend time reflecting on the day's activities. Such is the diversity of their characters that it isn't as simple as allocating a "slot" to devote to each child.

Whereas Indi loves me to give her my undivided attention, chatting till the cows come home, Noah won't sit still long enough, as kicking a ball around with him is more his love language. Ruby's always on a mission, a busy bee purposefully setting about her tasks with efficiency and pace, so it's usually best to join in with her. Elle is an incredibly helpful child with wisdom and maturity beyond her years, and sometimes she needs to be reminded to just go and dance without having a baby on her hips. Levi is my shadow who sticks with me like a faithful friend, and out of all of the little Smiths he's usually the one that gets more than his share of quality time—he's such a charmer. He loves nothing better than visiting Grandma's house, sipping milk, and eating chocolate.

One time Levi and Grandma had a falling-out about something, and Levi, mortified that he had upset Grandma, did his best to rectify the situation: "Grandma," he said, as if butter wouldn't melt in his mouth, "I must say what a beautiful dress you're wearing today." That was enough to send Grandma into peals of laughter. That day she happened to be wearing a pair of trousers.

Mary loves her books and raises her voice above everyone else's (even when no one else is actually around!) to get me to sit down and read a story with her. She comes to life when her brothers and sisters are around and has a great sense of humour.

Martin and I make it a priority to spend one-on-one time with the children. This could be a cycle ride to the beach or a milkshake moment. In our big family it's vital to make time for undivided attention, and we pull out all the stops to do this as equally and fairly as we can.

How do you manage the school run?

Journeying to and from school requires a system. So I keep the youngest two in the double stroller—firstly, so I know where they are, and secondly, so I have somewhere to put the bulky creations that come out of class. I encourage the older children to carry their own bags and coats. Noah learned this responsibility the tough way when he left his rucksack on the conveyor belt at Heathrow Airport. We'd made it all the way to the taxi line when he realised it was gone, so he and Martin had to dash back to find the lonely bag propped up against the luggage carousel. When Martin is away, my guardian angel, otherwise called Pip, picks up the older children in the morning. She's a massive help and makes my mornings a whole lot easier.

What about bedtime and sleep?

In descending order, the best sleepers in my household are as follows:

Noah is a brilliant sleeper and will actually request to go to bed. This sporty, active child is well and truly ready for slumber when bedtime arrives. A thumb in his mouth is Noah's tired signal.

Elle has never really been a difficult sleeper. She's fantastic at playing mum and will help bathe and read stories to the younger ones. She'll become extra helpful around bedtime, especially if visitors are around, and will use tactical methods to prolong the staying-up time—such as sudden urges to empty the dishwasher. Generally she'll keep a low profile and try to enter into the conversations with whomever is on the couch. However, I'm not too strict on this curfew as she's the eldest and I want to give her some special one-on-one time without the others. Besides, she's a great conversationalist and just beautiful company.

Levi is the one out of my brood who'll pick the longest story and will insist that I climb up into his bed to read it with him—he relishes one-to-one time. Out will come the stories of playground dramas and who cried in class—he saves up the whole day until bedtime so we can debrief.

Ruby is a woman on a mission, so she is pretty tired when bedtime arrives. Despite protestations about "not being tired," she's quite good at going down but can have interrupted sleep in the wee, small hours of the night.

As a newborn she had whooping cough for weeks on end. She's still the one with whom I'm up in the middle of the night, and as tempting as it is, especially when Martin's away, I try to settle her again in her cot and not bring her into my bed.

Indi is our night bird, the social butterfly that springs into life after hours—get me a massive dose of patience and a sleeping strategy that works. She's the one who'll think of umpteen reasons to justify coming down the stairs again: "More water, please," "It's too dark," "My knee hurts," "I found this toy for you," "I'm hungry," "Not tired," or "Can you get this hair band out of my hair?" The list is endless, and she has unlimited amounts of courage and lacks any fear of consequences. She's also the late sleeper in the morning who just can't get up and often faces a last-minute rush to get her uniform on and hair plaited.

What do you do when the bedtime methods don't work?

I've tried the "stay calm" approach, the "silent, no eye contact, shut the door, and repeat twenty times" approach. I've tried lying with them on the bed, stroking them, letting them listen to audio stories. I've tried the "5, 4, 3, 2, 1 countdown" tactic, where at 1 they're scampering up the stairs, as my tone gets lower and more assertive. I've tried penalties: no treats, no parties. I've tried it all. Seriously, there are times when I've felt desperate, tired, and home alone. *Is it too much to ask for just a minute to have to myself?*

Once, after exhausting every method in the book, I watched a program on TV called *Nanny 911,* on which they toss out advice and come back to angelic children in a week's time. One particular episode drew my attention because the featured child wouldn't go to bed. After flaunting all the tried and tested strategies that had failed for me, I was intrigued at the final approach. The nanny resorted to holding the bedroom door closed so the child simply couldn't get out. It wasn't really my style, but nothing else had worked, so I thought I'd give it a go.

The next night, there I was holding the door while one of my children screamed and screamed, pushing the door from the other side. It was a horrible end to the day, seemed to be a disastrous approach, and left us both in a puddle of tears.

The following day, I was on my way to church, bundling the children into the car, when for reasons that I fail to remember I got so cross with the same child, I took her into the kitchen, closed the glass door, and reminded the child of how angry I was.

As I held the door, with adrenalin pumping through my veins, I caught a glimpse of fear in her eyes as she and I held the door handle in a tug of war. At this moment I saw the fear that would have been the same behind the door the previous night—the feeling of being trapped in a room—and I realised how damaging it could be. I flung the door open, knelt beside her, and hugged her, apologising. Here I learned to trust my instincts. So I keep trying new things—at the moment, listening to music while going to sleep is working well.

What do you do when it gets tough?

Life's not easy, and we all know it can be tough. This is true if you're a CEO of a large business, a musician on the road, or a stay-at-home mum. Just keep going! Just because things are difficult doesn't mean that they're not right. Sometimes it's easy to assume that if something's going wrong, it must be for a reason. But I've found that character is developed during tough times, and dependency on God is there for me when I'm struggling.

My motto is to never give up and always keep running because "those who hope in the LORD will renew their strength.… They will run and not grow weary, they will walk and not be faint" (Isa. 40:31). This is a great promise to me when I'm flagging and life is tough and I feel like I'm walking in sinking sand. Sometimes I wonder why some people are destroyed by shaky times and others rise up strong and victorious. I think it all depends on where your heart is—God is more interested in the formation of my character than the situation I'm in. To be winners, we need to survive in a tough world, to practice self-control and compassion, to be servant-hearted and kind to everyone we meet, because people are all facing their own battles. Jesus was moved to compassion when He was in the midst of the suffering. He saw the large crowds and "he had compassion on them" (Matt. 14:14). Jesus didn't watch from the sidelines; He got in amidst the people.

How do you make time for each other?

The most important thing a wife can do for her child is to love her child's father. The most important thing a husband can do for his child is to love his child's mother. Keeping a relationship alive while raising a family is—*let's face it*—a juggling act, irrespective of how many children you have.

Marriage is not an extension of single life, and children shouldn't be the reason that a relationship dwindles from cruising in fifth gear to struggling in second gear. The statistics of marriages ending in divorce are frightening, so it's essential to nurture your marriage. No one intends for a collapse of a union, and yet so many times, marriage, for one reason or another, can be neglected.

About eight years into our marriage I remember struggling with issues of communication. We booked some time with a counsellor friend, got to the root of the problem, and moved forward—*it was so helpful*. We had to shake off pride and the stigma of going to someone who had expertise in this area. This was our marriage—no one else's—and we didn't want to settle for second best; we wanted it to be the best it could be (and still do!), so spending time with a counsellor wasn't a big deal. So I ask myself what safeguards I can use up to stop that from happening again, to keep my love alive, to conquer the tough times, and celebrate the good. And it doesn't just happen.

I liken it to a shop: The window display represents the beginning of the relationship in which everything looks exciting and inviting, then you step into the shop where you get involved at a more committed and more dedicated level. But the area that isn't visible, the real place where everything happens, is in the back. This is where the hard work takes place. Having only been married for fifteen years, I still find the window display very appealing. However, the reality can often be very different. I invite you to our breakfast table on a typical morning: I'm dealing with changing the baby's diaper while the phone is ringing, and Levi is arguing with Noah about who has the most Cheerios in their bowl. The school year is upon us, and field-trip money and consent slips need to be filled in and sent to the school.

My need for assistance often coincides with Martin's creative juices flowing and, "Not now, Anna, I'm creating a symphony in my head!" I try to accept this with gracious ears, but sometimes the words "Sure, honey," elude me. At times like these the window display isn't helpful, but the deep commitment and depth of our relationship sustains us. We are still learning daily!

As Martin is often away, the time that he spends in our home is precious. Somewhere between fighting the jet lag, processing the slums of India, giving interviews, recording in the studio, and handling all the day-to-day busyness, even having coffee together is a beautiful thing. My number-one rule is: Keep realistic expectations. A romantic lunch for two may sound amazing, but with children squeezing onto my lap or constructing a train set under my feet, we would get frustrated. Every child wants a little bit of attention, though some vocalise it more than others. But how do I save time for the love of my life?

For Martin and me, the parental relationship is so demanding that when we're tired or stressed we have to make time for one another. There are times when our relationship feels strained, when attentions are divided, energy levels plummet, and sleep is disturbed. Sometimes the thought of a night of passion is, well, just left as a thought, because a decent night's sleep becomes music to our ears.

Communication is so vital in these situations: talking, laughing, keeping a sense of humour, acknowledging the season of life that we're in, and refusing to allow a spiral of discontent and bitterness. We try to voice our thoughts and feelings and understand each other's needs, but when this doesn't happen arguments start and resentment can breed.

In the hustle and bustle of family life it's important to keep love alive with affection. Touch is probably the earliest sense that we develop and has a powerful effect on how we react to a situation, both with my family and with my man. Kissing, holding, embracing, and tickling— all are so valuable. Positive touch can give a message of affirmation, love, and security, and a hug is one of the most affirming nonverbal messages that we can give each other—it communicates value and worth and doesn't cost a penny. Almost instinctively in a time of crisis, we hug one another because a hug is an instant and powerful communicator of love. Jesus affirmed others with His touch through healing and compassion. Nonsexual touch and affection as a husband and wife is vital in the family unit, sending a strong positive message of love and security. Instead of playing down physical affection, we deliberately celebrate it by expressing it in front of our children (within reason!).

How Martin and I interact as husband and wife models love for our children, and this model will stay with them long into their adult life and into their own relationships. And we don't apologise to the children when we need our own space. Sometimes they need to know that they can't come first every time.

How do you make time for you?

This won't take long! A hot bubble bath is hard to beat. I love going to the hairdresser—I tell her to do whatever with my hair, and I just enjoy the chance to sit down and read a magazine. If there's a party, I'm there (any excuse to dress up, even if it's for an open evening at school). The gym? I have a love/hate relationship with this place—I'm not sure what I think of it really. Surely I keep fit enough running around after the children? I'm not somebody who craves time on my own, but I love getting out of the house at least once a day even if it's pouring rain and all the children are home. You may wonder how on earth this book ever got to print (so do I!). It's taken a while! I don't have six children with me all day, so there are pockets of time where I can catch up on email and grab a coffee. Note to self: When the baby is sleeping, I must resist the urge to busy myself with the things I can do when she's awake.

What about spending time with God?

I struggled with this for many years, feeling bad that I didn't have daily "quiet time." I now get the "Word of the Day" emailed to my phone, which I pick up at the start of each day. Also, I read my "Bible in a Year" each night before I go to sleep. I use different props to pray for things throughout the day—so when I'm polishing the children's school shoes I pray for their day in the classroom, and if I see a pregnant lady in the supermarket I remember to pray for my friends who are expecting. I love the way the Holy Spirit uses familiar things to prompt me to speak to God about my life. However, the hardest part is stopping and listening to God—so I try and remember to "be still" and know that God is God at some stage during the hectic part of my day.

How do you manage when Martin's away?

Martin uses his passport more than the children use their library cards! Twelve years of marriage, hundreds of gigs later, and thousands of air miles travelled, and you'd think that the sight of that little black suitcase would get easier. It doesn't.

I've used my own coping strategies while Martin is away, my own routines, which provide stability and normality in the children's lives. Usually I take on a mini project that I challenge myself to do before he returns home. Also, living within such a tight-knit community where I can walk to my sisters' houses is enormously reassuring, and although we might not always fit into each other's daily schedules, knowing they're there is very comforting. Such is the regularity of the trips that the children, although sad when Daddy leaves for another country, remain incredibly resilient and bounce back by the time

Martin has reached the petrol station at the top of our road! They understand that this is Daddy's job and know no different. Having all their cousins in the same boat at school, Sunday school, clubs, and social events has helped too. And it's an added bonus if Daddy leaves a little note for them under their pillow to find at bedtime.

ACKNOWLEDGEMENTS

To my best friend and love of my life, Mart. This book would never have been finished without your encouragement and support. I love you. (PS: I hope I didn't reveal too much!)

Our six beautiful children: Elle-Anna, Noah, Indi-Anna, Levi, Ruby-Anna, and Mary-Anna. You make us laugh and cry, but most of all you complete our family. We adore you and are so proud of all of you.

To my amazing mum, Heather. I have modelled my life on the way you have been as a mum. Thank you for always being there for me. You are a constant support, a fantastic grandma, and someone I can laugh, cry, and eat a cheese scone with!

To my beautiful dad, David; Tim and Becca; Stew and Sarah; Jon and Kristen; and Ben. You guys rock! To my in-laws, Eddie and Sylvia; Paul and Pip; Pete and Alison; and Suzi and Giles. You are ALL amazing. Thanks for being there and seeing Mart and me through this season full of peaks and troughs. To all my gorgeous nieces and nephews: I love you all so much, and God loves you more than you know.

To the Delirious? family. What a journey we have been on together. Through the highs and lows we fought through. Those amazing memories of doing life together on tour buses will stay with us forever, I'm sure. Guys, you always went the extra mile to reach people who needed reaching and to show God's love and grace to all we met. I love you all.

I would love to mention all my close friends at Arun Community Church—you all know who you are.... I have learnt so much from you all and am forever grateful for your kindness and friendship.

To Jess Bee: Thank you for your valuable editing help. To Alex, Amy, Chris, Caitlyn, and all at David C Cook. Thanks for believing in this book and for putting it in the hands of people. You have been amazing to work with.

There have been so many friends who have helped and inspired me to write this book, who have all been a part of the story that's been written: Darlene and Mark; Tim and Rachel; Matt and Beth; Jim McNeish; Liz Warom; Roy Baylis; Hoda and Laura; Stella Coulter (my right-hand lady); Flory Fuller and Eszter Szarvas (my amazing au pairs); Lottie and Sim; Tracy and Jamie; Andy and Pippa; Jeff and Jess; Tony and Terri; the bigEye girls—Tash, Steph, and Toria ... you helped me to dream bigger; Nicola Holmes and all the girls in the playground.

And last but not least: the amazing Caz Johnson. We did it!! I never dreamt or believed it would happen, but together we did it. I have been so incredibly privileged to know such an amazing woman of God as you. Caz, you are a true inspiration to me; you can pack more into an hour than most can in a day! I stand amazed. I love you, girl.

Finally, thanks be to God, my heavenly Father. You continually save me.